HOPING LIBERIA

STORIES OF CIVIL WAR FROM AFRICA'S FIRST REPUBLIC

Michael Helms

Smyth & Helwys Publishing, Inc.
6316 Peake Road
Macon, Georgia 31210-3960
1-800-747-3016
©2009 by Smyth & Helwys Publishing
All rights reserved.
Printed in the United States of America.

The paper used in this publication meets the minimum requirements of
American National Standard for Information Sciences—
Permanence of Paper for Printed Library Materials.
ANSI Z39.48–1984. (alk. paper)

Library of Congress Cataloging-in-Publication Data

Helms, John Michael.

Hoping Liberia : stories of civil war from Africa's first republic / by John Michael Helms. p. cm.
Includes bibliographical references (p.) and index.
ISBN 978-1-57312-544-4 (pbk. : alk. paper)
1. Christian sociology—Liberia.
2. Liberia—Social conditions.
3. Menjay, Olu.
I. Title. BR1463.L7H46 2009 286'.1666209049—dc22 2009038675

Hoping Liberia

Stories of Civil War *from*
Africa's First Republic

John Michael
Helms

Praise for *Hoping Liberia*

Ricks Institute and Olu Menjay—a struggling school and a committed Christian—are together making a huge contribution to the restoration of previously war-torn Liberia. Ricks and Olu have captured the hearts and pocketbooks of a number of Christians and churches in our country. But no person has been more passionate for the support and success of Ricks than Michael Helms. An inspiring book about hope, *Hoping Liberia* is also a magic story of Christian stewardship.

—**Dr. Walter B. Shurden**
Minister at Large, Mercer University

Hoping Liberia is an inspiring work in every way. It tells a story, not just about what God is doing among Christians in Liberia, but also about the way God has tugged on Michael Helms's heart and changed him and many others through their friendship with and service alongside Christian brothers and sisters in Liberia. This book indeed brought me much hope; maybe we Baptists can once again be known for our love and service and not for our fighting and politics. I strongly recommend *Hoping Liberia*.

—**Dr. David P. Gushee**
Distinguished University Professor of Christian Ethics
McAfee School of Theology at Mercer University

In past generations God has raised up Baptists in the South with prophetic voices on the matter of racial reconciliation, such as T. B. Matson, Henlee Barnett, Foy Valentine, and John H. Claypool. Today, it is John Michael Helms. While this book reads like a novel, it is a well-researched history of Liberia, reaching back to the slave trade with its attendant evils, which Helms makes fresh and revealing. We see how "the sins of the fathers have planted sour grapes so that the children's teeth have been set on edge." In addition to its prophetic voice, *Hoping Liberia* is insightful, purposeful, and missional and will move the reader into "*missio Dei.*"

—**Dr. Emmanuel McCall**
Founding Pastor of The Fellowship Group
East Point, Georgia

Every good story needs a good storyteller. The story of Olu Menjay and Ricks Institute is a very good story. Michael Helms is a very good storyteller. Now the story will be shared far and wide. Thanks be to God for the story and its teller.

—Dr. Richard F. Wilson
Columbus Roberts Professor of Theology and
Chair, Roberts Department of Christianity, Mercer University

In *Hoping Liberia*, Michael Helms weaves together multiple stories—the story of his friendship with Olu Menjay, the director of Ricks Institute in Virginia, Liberia; the story of their partnership in ministry; and the story of the nation of Liberia. Through historical narrative, theological ponderings, personal confession, and thoughtful questions, Helms immerses readers into a period of political turmoil and violence, a devastating civil war, and the immeasurable suffering experienced by the Liberian people. In the midst of the aftermath of these harsh realities, Liberian Christians held on to hope, and *Hoping Liberia* is ultimately an inspirational and uplifting story of faith being lived out and the body of Christ coming together and joining hands to do God's work.

—Dr. Pamela R. Durso
Executive Director, Baptist Women in Ministry
Atlanta, Georgia

Also by John Michael Helms

*Finding Our Way: An Introspective Journey
through the Labyrinth of Life*

In Memoriam

Dedicated to
Connie Mobley and John M. Mobley, Sr.,
who lived lives of significance.

The slave trade, which African and African-American scholars sometimes call the "Maafa" (meaning "holocaust"), affected between 9 and 12 million people. The fourteen-year civil war in Liberia killed between 250,000 and 300,000 people, about 1 in 10 Liberians. This book is dedicated to their memory. The labor on this book is on behalf of Ricks Institute in Virginia, Liberia, and of approximately 1,000 refugees of the war who still live on the Ricks campus.

Acknowledgments

I must begin by thanking the mission-minded people of Clarkesville Baptist Church in Clarkesville, Georgia, for sending Olu Menjay and me to Liberia in 1995. Without their openness to the Holy Spirit's movement in our lives, the trip would never have occurred. As you shall see, the trip came at an important time in Olu's life, which God later used in many ways. The trip also became a point of entry for my ministry in Liberia, which I believe will continue indefinitely.

Secondly, I thank the members of Trinity Baptist Church in Moultrie, Georgia, for granting me a sabbatical to go to Liberia in 2006. After I accepted a job as this congregation's pastor in 1996, they agreed to grant me a sabbatical after each five years of service. My trip to Liberia was the second sabbatical of my tenure.

I received a grant through the Cooperative Baptist Fellowship (CBF), which helped with some of the expenses of my sabbatical. CBF has several excellent planning resources and ideas for assisting clergy and churches in planning sabbaticals. I am grateful for the assistance I received from CBF in planning both of my sabbaticals, especially the one to Liberia.

I appreciate Trinity Baptist for sending a work team the following year— including Ellen and Farrell Tucker, Pat Tomlinson, John and Ryan Helms, and me—to Ricks Institute to help supply water to the school's campus. I'll never forget the joy on the faces of the cooks as they saw water flow into the kitchen for the first time in more than fifteen years and the excitement of students and teachers as toilets were flushed in the school. No longer were students required to relieve themselves in the tall grass or the filthy latrines.

I also thank the members of Trinity for the honor of being their pastor for thirteen years. The longevity of pastors at Trinity is a testimony to the love these people have for one another and their ministers, the desire and ability of ministers and laity to work toward common kingdom goals, and the quality of living within this community.

I appreciate Dr. Walter Shurden (Buddy) for breaking bread with me at a restaurant in Macon and listening to me talk about my book. I had written five chapters and hoped I could convince him to read them. The chapters were all historical. After hearing me talk passionately about Liberia and my experiences with Olu, Buddy told me I needed to write the stories and allow the history to work in the background. "If you are writing for the laity, they don't read history," he said. Coming from one of our foremost Baptist historians, that shocked me. My visit with him saved my project. I believe he kept my work from being added to the long list of books few people want to read.

I took my five chapters home and started again. I didn't even ask Buddy to read the originals. However, my visit freed me. I began writing with fresh joy and abandonment. Stubbornly, I still chose to include some historical content, but I wrote them in a narrative form. Liberian history is enmeshed with American history and Christian theology. It's not possible to understand the Liberian civil war without some understanding of the part both history and theology played in the lives of Liberians.

I thank Dr. Olu Menjay for being my long-distance friend, for reviewing the manuscript, and for his ideas and suggestions on the project. Olu helps me stay balanced. He reminds me not to let the material things become too important. After spending a month in Liberia, I found it difficult to come back to America and live the same way without thinking of those I know who live with almost nothing.

In following God's direction to return to Liberia, Dr. Menjay has been richly blessed with a beautiful family. He found a beautiful bride, Ottolee Moncy Menjay. On June 4, 2007, they were blessed with their first child, a daughter they named Orlaine Mia Menjay. The blessing of a son, Olu Q. Menjay, Jr., arrived on June 18, 2009, and they call him "Q." The Menjay children represent the post-civil war generation, which we hope will know about war only from the stories told by the generations that come before them.

I thank the faculty and students of Ricks Institute. While living among them for several weeks, I listened as many of them talked freely about their experiences during the war. I went to their homes and worshiped in their churches. They treated me as an honored guest. These people have my highest respect for the work they do at the school and the faith they maintain in the midst of difficult surroundings.

While I have the gifts to frame thoughts and ideas, I needed lots of help in cleaning up these pages. My group of proofreaders included Zach Dawes, Jr., who came to Trinity Baptist as minister of education and outreach through the Cooperative Baptist Fellowship's Resident Program. Zach is a graduate of Baylor and Truett Seminary. He has a sharp mind and a good eye for detail. Zach made helpful observations and suggestions as I worked.

My mother, Lenora Helms, a retired schoolteacher, also aided me as I strove to improve the manuscript.

Three other women did the bulk of the work. Misti Cato, church secretary, and Charlotte Sellers, office manager, have served at Trinity for thirteen and fifteen years respectively. The church is blessed to have them. Misti and Charlotte read the manuscript before passing it on to the queen of all proofreaders, Andrea Savage. Andrea has a Ph.D. in English, so she's highly capable. Her father, a retired Baptist pastor and a gifted writer himself, once commented that she has "correction fluid running through her veins." She has been nicer to me than I deserve. Andrea proofed my weekly article for the *Moultrie Observer* for nine years. She gives me the confidence I need to write, knowing that, with her help, my work is going to be free of most errors. I am thankful to God for her. She helped make the project possible, as she did for my first book, *Finding Our Way—An Introspective Journey through the Labyrinth of Life.*

Once the book found its way to the publisher, Leslie Andres became my shepherd. As the editor on this project, she guided me with valuable insight, made strategic changes, and gave the book the critique it needed to make it a better read. Then, under a very tight deadline, Dr. Diana Young, a member of First Baptist Church in Jefferson, scanned for errors in a final read.

Finally, I am grateful to the people of First Baptist Church of Jefferson, Georgia, for calling me as their pastor in June 2009. As we find our way together, I am joining them in the good ministry they already do in Jefferson, Jackson County, and other places, and I hope to help them find their way to new places of ministry such as Liberia and other parts of the world.

—John Michael Helms
July 2009

Contents

*Returning from church, Dr. Olu and Mrs. Ottolee Menjay
on the campus of Ricks Institute.*

Foreword

Frustration, hardship, sufferings, conflict, violence, deprivation, and hopelessness are real conditions people face daily around the world. These conditions are so real that sometimes the potential to hope for a better day is farfetched.

It was in the thick of the rainy season in 1990 when the rebels of the National Patriotic Front of Liberia, headed by Charles Taylor, captured the Old Road and Airfield areas of Monrovia, the capital of Liberia. At age eighteen, I was in that area seeking safety in the home of a pastor. I had been separated from my family for a few months. My parents had fled the Gardnersville area where we lived toward the New Kru Town-Bushrod Island in search of food and security.

The rebels, dressed in mischief clothing and masks and carrying automatic machine guns, demanded that all persons residing in the Old Road and Airfield areas move towards Paynesville-Duport Road. Many of the rebels were far younger than I. The journey from Old Road to Duport Road was hopeless. The music of persistent gunfire, the stench of dead bodies, and the unbelievable scene of murdered babies and children quickly led me to the conclusion that my life was going to end in a few hours or days. Frankly, I felt I was living without life.

When we got to Duport Road, we had to go through a dangerous rebels' checkpoint, where the rebels painstakingly interrogated everyone. Some in our company were taken from the exodus and shot with automatic rifles. It was so bloodcurdling! During the journey from Duport Road to Soul Cleaning Mission (a Christian mission center housing internally displaced people), we had to walk through a swamp flooded not only with rainwater, but with floating dead bodies.

What follows next when one is engulfed with such hopeless conditions?

There must be value placed in cultivating relationships if we are to build a sustaining Liberia. Relationships with our peers, with others both locally and internationally, go a long way in building a sustainable life.

What spared my life then and sustains my life of service to others now was a critical recognition of the importance of relationships. I was spared the executioner's bullet simply because I spoke my name, Olu Menjay. One of the rebel guards heard the name and intervened. He had known my father, Harrison Menjay, and knew that my father was a man of compassion and encouragement. The good name of my father saved my life and set me on the path of doing what I can to save the lives of others.

Frankly, apart from relationships I have built over the years, it is almost impossible to study, serve, and share in my own experience. If Liberia is to be hoped, we must invest in relationships that encourage and support us in unusual ways.

Hoping Liberia: Stories of Civil War from Africa's First Republic is a biography of living in the absence of hope while refusing to accept the notion of despair.

In the face of the horror of Apartheid, Archbishop Desmond Tutu commented, "In South Africa it is impossible to be optimistic. Therefore it is necessary to hope." The conditions of South Africa were horrible, but South Africa was spared the unspeakable horrors of civil war. Tutu's insight is only magnified in the context of Liberia's journey through deep darkness.

We must never give up in the midst of the worst conditions of living. As a student at Mercer University, attending Sunday morning services at First Baptist Church of Christ in Macon, Georgia, I often heard then-preacher Dr. Chuck Poole say, "The worst thing is never the last thing in God's world." Indeed, the worst conditions in life must never be our concluding notion of our life. The final condition of our experience must be enshrined with hope and possibilities. This book describes the ways in which a simple leap of faith can restore our seemingly hopeless world and circumstances.

This book encourages investment in rebuilding dreams and hope. It offers anecdotes that are historical as well as personal. It points the readers to the real meaning of hope amid life's difficulties. There is nothing so important in life as our investment in hope. This book demands the human spirit to invest in efforts that are sustaining.

A tangible investment in hope as described in this book is the Ricks Institute, a school destroyed and looted during the nearly fifteen years of war in Liberia. Ricks Institute now offers a sustaining future for Liberia through its provision of quality education to the girls and boys who are the future leaders of Liberia and our world. A special lesson taught at Ricks each day is the essence of living with integrity in the midst of challenges. The meaning of life draws its nourishment from hope.

In our extreme sufferings and challenges, it is not so easy to speak of hope or to encourage the conversation on being hopeful. When I arrived at Ricks to serve as the principal in 2005 (right after the civil war), the challenges overshadowed any apparent potential at the school. The deplorable conditions were physical and psychological; they were visible and heartbreaking. I insisted within my heart that in these circumstances, there must be at least minimum and positive signposts of possibilities. Then I realized that our signposts of hope and possibilities at Ricks were the girls and boys. We started to invest and see the potential of our community through the children who attend the school. While we have struggled with the physical scars, we have been encouraged by the potential in the children.

Realizing the "*what could be*" in a person does not happen easily. One has to commit to being patient and humble. One must invest in the seemingly insignificant, minor matters. It is the mundane things and the "*what could be*" in life that order our future.

We are indebted to Michael Helms for the way he articulates our story and the history of Liberia. Dr. Helms, over the years of our evolving friendship, always thought that my story should be made public. I wrestled with making my story of pain, struggle, and hope public simply because of the so-called value I placed on confidentiality. My story is only a small part of the hurtful realities of so many people who died and who survived the circumstances in Liberia.

The simple themes and lessons within the stories and the reflective engagements called "Hoping Small Groups" at the end of the book join the convictions that God is present in our stories and that God's presence matters in our search for hope.

May this book encourage readers to see that personal stories have the promise to uncover our pain and point our focus to a hopeful future. *Hoping Liberia* is a springboard to encourage others to become faithful to hope in the face of even dreadful realities.

—Olu Q. Menjay, Sr.
Ricks Institute
Virginia, Liberia
Rainy Season

Introduction

Where does hope begin? Strangely enough, hope begins with depravity. We do not hope unless we are without. If we have it, we don't hope for it, whatever "it" might be.

If we dare to dream, then hope grows from depravity. Dreaming takes us beyond our limitations and into worlds of new possibility. Early American slaves dreamed of being set free from their masters and living a life of freedom. Memories and freedom stories that survived generation after generation fueled those dreams, supplying the kindling needed to keep the fires of hope burning. Hope survived despite little evidence that freedom would ever be possible.

Paul wrote to the church at Rome, "But hope that is seen is no hope at all. Who hopes for what he already has? But if we hope for what we do not yet have, we wait for it patiently" (Rom 8:24-25, NIV).

When people cease to wait patiently and finally give up on their dreams, hope dies. Even people of faith can develop doubts about God's power or sovereignty. Ishmael was born because Sarah and Abraham believed their hopes of having a child the way God promised were dead. Some grow angry with God; others become apathetic and their faith atrophies, sometimes to the point that it flickers out like a dying ember.

Technically, hope also dies when it is fulfilled, like a seed dies when the life within pushes forth. Like a caterpillar that spins into a cocoon and later emerges as a moth, hope also dies when it is transformed. The old has gone and the new has come. Like the cicada leaving behind its shell, we discard fulfilled hope. We take wing to explore new possibilities.

God is always calling people to bring a hopeful message to the sick, to those in prison, to the oppressed, to the poor, to the young, to the old, to the dying, to the depressed, to those struggling with addiction, to the unloved, to those in refugee camps, to those without health insurance, to the illiterate, to the unemployed, to those denied human rights, to people on the move, to the hungry, to those without shelter, to those without fresh and safe drinking water, to the grieving, to the childless, and to the lonely. To all of these people and more, God sends hope. Hope arrives through the encouraging words and hopeful actions of those who are moved enough to help relieve suffering in the name of Jesus.

Americans understand that our nation is the most blessed on earth. Despite our country's problems, the disadvantaged of this world still want to come to America. Throughout the Liberian civil war, America became a haven for more than 100,000 Liberians. Many of these were eventually granted green cards and allowed to remain in our country. Understandably, few returned to Liberia. This is a story of one who *has* returned to his homeland, Liberia, to bring a message of hope—Dr. Olu Menjay.

When Mother Teresa first went to work with the poor of Calcutta, India, it's not likely her decision made any news. In fact, who could say they knew Nënë Tereza Agnes Gonxhe Bojaxhiu of Albania in 1950? Only after her years and years of labor with the poorest of the poor did anyone begin to notice.

The work of Mother Teresa with the poor in Calcutta influenced Dr. Olu Menjay to return to his home country and work with the poor, the uneducated, the homeless, and the people whose hope was lost during the fourteen-year civil war. He decided that living a life of significance was more important than living a life of success as typically defined in America.

Raised by Christian parents, including a father who was a Baptist pastor in Nimba and later in Monrovia, Liberia, Olu embraced and appreciated his Baptist heritage. After coming within a moment of being executed during the beginning months of the Liberian civil war, he felt deep gratitude toward God for sparing his life. After living as a refugee for nearly two years in the Ivory Coast, he had a deep appreciation for shelter and daily bread. After receiving an opportunity from a Southern Baptist missionary to travel to the United States to study, he appreciated education. After returning to Liberia with me in 1995, being ordained to the gospel ministry, and seeing his father for the last time, he appreciated the gifts of blessing, family, and the voice of the church in the midst of the greatest crisis in his nation's history.

In *Hoping Liberia—Stories of Civil War from Africa's First Republic*, Dr. Olu Menjay, a graduate of Truett McConnell College, Mercer University, Duke Divinity School, Boston University, and the University of Wales (International Baptist Theological Seminary) in Prague, Czech Republic, will challenge you with his dedication and desire to invest his life among the people of his homeland.

As a gifted preacher and teacher, he could have stayed in America and lived comfortably, but he could not have transmitted hope to Liberians as he stood at American pulpits and taught in American classrooms. As young Rev. Menjay contemplated his future, God's call eventually resonated clearly, and he knew he should return and *hope* Liberia.

If use the phrase "hope Liberia" intentionally. I have often heard older people in the South interchange the words "hope" and "help." My grandfather did this many times. He might say something like, "Mr. Green hoped me keep my cows fed while I was gone." So imagine my surprise when I was in Liberia, an English-speaking country, and I heard this same idiom used by Dr. Menjay.

As he stood in the chapel service on our mission team's final day in Liberia, he said, "Students, today we want to thank the mission team from Trinity Baptist Church in Moultrie, Georgia, U.S.A., for coming to Liberia and hoping us at Ricks Institute."

I can only surmise that freed slaves brought the idiom over on their return ships. They were people with dreams of a new land with new opportunities—no more chains, no more masters, no more beatings, and no more forced labor. The idiom, which is often used in Liberia, must have been passed down through the generations and survived tucked away in pockets of Liberian speech, as it does in pockets of American speech today.

When someone says, "Help me," it's a way of saying, "Unless you help me I am without hope." When someone says, "Hope me," it's a way of saying, "The way you give me hope is by giving me some help."

Throughout this book, you will notice that the word "hope" is used in place of the word "help," just as Dr. Menjay used it in chapel that day, and just as I'm using it in the title of this book and in the "Hoping Small Group" section. I want to remind the reader that unless help comes, hope often dies.

Hoping Liberia chronicles God's ongoing work to restore hope to the students in and around Virginia, Liberia, specifically, to the students of Ricks Institute, a boarding school established in 1887. *Hoping Liberia* is the unfinished story of Dr. Olu Menjay and his faculty who are rebuilding hopes and dreams of children and teenagers in war-torn Liberia in a school that was once the premier boarding school in that country. They do their work through strong academics within a Christian environment, sharing the love of Jesus and preaching the gospel.

To help readers better understand the interconnected stories of Dr. Menjay's life, the Ricks Institute, and my experiences in Liberia, I have provided a basic history of Liberia and connected the dots, I hope, from that point to the Liberian civil war and the reasons for the erosion of hope within the country. I make a case that the destructive forces at work in the civil war can be traced like a recessive gene back to the American slave trade, from which the attitude of superiority of one race over another was handed down to the freed slaves who settled the western shores of Africa, which later became Liberia. Upon settling the West African coastline, these freed slaves, known as Americo-Liberians, imposed their hand of domination on the indigenous population for more than 150 years, leading to rising tensions that eventually culminated in the assassination of President William Tolbert in 1979. From there the country spiraled out of control, and the civil war began a decade later.

Hope is like currency. We can invest hope and watch it multiply with interest for future generations, or we can run a hope deficit that future generations will have to pay. Liberia is paying today for the sins of her fathers. Indeed, she is paying for sins that reach as far back as the American slave trade.

Hope, or the lack of it, works that way, too. A generation can learn to be hopeful from the generation before it, or it can also lose hope because of the previous generation. This is the reason people like Dr. Olu Menjay are so important to Liberia. He inspires, teaches, energizes, and encourages today's Liberian youth. He builds tomorrow's leaders. He works to convince them that their generation doesn't have to be like the generation before them. Without people like Dr. Menjay returning to his native land to tell the children that all things are possible through Christ who gives them strength, who is going to *hope* Liberia?

Dr. Menjay has inspired me. I believe strongly in what he is doing. I believe one person can make a difference in the world. I have seen firsthand that Dr. Olu Menjay makes a difference in Liberia. He is not alone. Many choose to join hands with him to raise a new generation of leaders for Liberia. All who join hands with Ricks Institute receive as much blessing, if not more, than those at Ricks. We discover the truth of Acts 20:35: "It is more blessed to give than to receive" (NIV).

Many churches are helping Ricks Institute get back on its feet since Dr. Menjay became principal. These churches and institutions represent theological and racial diversity, but we have in common our love for missions and a strong belief in James 2:15-17: "What good is it, my brothers, if a man claims to have faith but has no deeds? Can such faith save him? Suppose a brother or sister is without clothes and daily food. If one of you says to him, 'Go, I wish you well; keep warm and well fed,' but does nothing about his physical needs, what good is it? In the same way, faith by itself, if it is not accompanied by action, is dead" (NIV).

The royalties from the sale of this book go to the Bricks for Ricks Liberian Housing Foundation, Inc., which I established to hope Ricks Institute and to hope relocate people who struggle to return to their places of origin but are hindered by the destruction of their homes and the dangerous memories associated with the trauma of being forced from their villages. We will assist them by building homes with bricks from a compressed earth brick-making machine, which compresses brick made from 90 percent soil and 10 percent cement. Once our compressed earth brick-making machine is purchased, these homes can be made cheaply, but will be strong enough to last for the next generation.

Readers will find specific information about helping Ricks Institute in the appendices. Appendix 1 offers instructions on how to donate to the Bricks for Ricks project. Appendix 2 provides information on accessing the Ricks Institute website and learning more about the work Dr. Menjay and the faculty are doing. Ways to donate your time, money, and talents to the school are also outlined.

I invite you to take a journey with me as I share Dr. Olu Menjay's story and other stories of the Liberian civil war, how Liberia fell into the war, why we should care, and how Dr. Menjay and others are currently *hoping Liberia.*

Chapter 1

The Value of a Good Name

"A man's name stays above the grave." —*African proverb*

December 1995

Our plane sat on a runway in Sierra Leone as the African sun baked us like potatoes. While we awaited takeoff, I looked at the small thermometer attached to my backpack: 87 degrees. I wasn't surprised. Sweat rolled down my face. My shirt was wringing wet. I twisted the overhead knobs once more in hopes of getting some air to flow. Nothing.

I looked around to gauge the reactions of the passengers. I could see beads of sweat popping out on their dark foreheads, but no one complained. Most sat quietly, while some carried on light conversations.

The small plane held about sixteen Liberians who were returning to the war-torn country for a brief stay. I wouldn't say the heat didn't bother them. They were all prepared for inconvenience, but perhaps not quite so soon.

The people on this plane knew well what they were returning to. Perhaps some would be surprised by the extent of the damage the war had done to their country, but there would be no culture shock like I was about to experience. They had seen the poverty and vast numbers of hungry, unemployed, and uneducated people before. Since the war began in 1989, those numbers had steadily increased. For many in Liberia, hope was sliding through their lives like the last few grains of sand sliding through an hourglass. For tens of thousands, hope had already died.

The flight from Sierra Leone was the last leg of a long trip. The difficulty of getting to Liberia reminded me of a saying I heard when I was younger: "You can't get there from here." It was usually said as a joke, but it also meant you had to travel to another place before you could get to where you wanted to go.

That described Liberia in December 1995. You couldn't get to Liberia from almost anywhere. The war had separated the country from most of the world. Only two flights per week carrying about sixteen passengers each went into and out of Liberia.

From my home in Clarkesville, Georgia, I traveled to Atlanta, Georgia. From Atlanta, I flew to New York City; then to Paris, France; then on to Dakar, Senegal; from Dakar to Abidjan, Ivory Coast; and from Abidjan to Monrovia, Liberia. Total elapsed time from my home in Clarkesville to the Liberian Baptist Compound was about two days, with a night's rest at a Southern Baptist missionary's residence in Abidjan.

My traveling companion was Olu Menjay, a native Liberian studying at Duke Divinity School. Olu was a recent graduate of Mercer University and also a graduate of Truett-McConnell Junior College in Cleveland, Georgia, about fifteen miles from Clarkesville Baptist Church where I served as pastor. He and other college students occasionally attended the church. He often stopped by my office when he passed through Clarkesville. We discussed life, school, and theology. Through these visits, I first heard Olu's compelling story.

The Struggles of a Liberian Youth

In 1971, Harrison and Ella Menjay, with their one-year-old son, Hugo, traveled from Liberia to Nigeria, where Harrison enrolled at Nigerian Baptist Theological Seminary, an opportunity made possible by the president of Liberia, William Tolbert. Soon thereafter, the Menjays' second son, Olu, was born at the Baptist Hospital in Ogbomoso.

Olu was two years old when his family returned to Liberia. Now ordained to the ministry, Rev. Harrison Menjay began pastoring a Baptist church and became principal of a junior high school in Nimba, northern Liberia. When Olu was ready for school, he attended St. Mary's Catholic School in Nimba. During the next several years, the Menjay family grew. Mrs. Menjay gave birth to another son and three daughters, a typical large Liberian family.

By the time Olu reached high school, his family had relocated to Monrovia, where Olu was educated at Suehn Mission, a boarding school supported by the Foreign Mission Board of the National Baptist Convention, USA, Inc.

Boarding schools were once common in Liberia. They made good sense for families, as transportation was difficult in such a poor country. Even so, it was still a financial sacrifice for parents to send their children to these schools in a country that offered few government-funded schools. For those who could afford them, boarding schools were a better choice to give children a good educational experience.

Olu completed all his high school course work and was awaiting graduation when tragedy struck Liberia. On Christmas Eve 1989, the nation erupted in civil war. However, this was not the first time in Olu's life when violence had marred his nation.

While there were other flash points of violence in Liberian history, an important benchmark of violence in its contemporary history is April 12, 1980, when Olu was a child. On the evening of April 11, President William Tolbert attended a religious concert at Providence Baptist Church. Instead of returning to his private residence several miles from the city, as was his custom, he went to his official residence and office at the executive mansion and fell asleep there. That night, a group of seventeen soldiers led by Master Sergeant Samuel Doe invaded the mansion, discovered the president sleeping, and killed him.

The morning after President Tolbert was killed, Samuel Doe went on the radio to announce the successful overthrow of the True Whig Party government. He became the first indigenous president of Liberia, claiming that his administration took the country on behalf of Liberia's indigenous people. In fear for their lives, many Americo-Liberians (descendants of freed American slaves who established the country's government, built the first schools, and brought the Christian religion to the region) immediately went into exile as the new government initially shared wealth of the coup with some of the indigenous people and held trial for leading members of President Tolbert's cabinet. Ten days after the assassination of the president, thirteen leading members of Tolbert's government were executed on the beach in Monrovia.

The assassination of President Tolbert was the culmination of more than a century and a half of deep-seated animosity between descendants of indigenous people groups of Liberia and descendants of the first Americo-Liberians.

At first, Doe was popular among the indigenous population, but his prominence waned in following years. It became apparent that this nearly illiterate man who came from the deepest part of Liberia's forest and belonged to the smallest of Liberia's sixteen tribes, the Khran people, did not have the skills to lead a nation. Opposition to his ten-year rule began to mount.

On Christmas Eve 1989, as Olu looked forward to high school graduation in early January 1990, an alliance of Liberians especially opposing Samuel Doe's dictatorship, united in the establishment of the National Patriotic Front of Liberia (NPFL). They invaded from the Ivory Coast under the leadership of Charles Taylor, a corrupt former civil servant under Doe who eventually became Liberia's twenty-second president.

Like tens of thousands of people in Monrovia and the surrounding areas, Olu became separated from his family as the fighting and violence increased. People sought refuge wherever possible. Every day presented a challenge for families to find

A road sign tells the story of one of Liberia's common crimes, especially during the war.

food, water, and shelter, and to avoid the rebels who could kill, rob, and rape at will.

Olu first sought refuge at the Liberian Baptist Theological Seminary, about twelve miles outside Monrovia. He had often visited with his father, so he knew many of the teachers there. He stayed for several weeks until the fighting moved too close. At this point, he hitchhiked further north to Roberts International Airport and hid in the Harbel region, named for the founder of the Firestone Tire and Rubber Company, Harvey S. Firestone, and his wife Idabelle.

In March 1990, Olu decided to take his chances. Leaving Liberia seemed like a better risk than staying. Hungry and tired, he gathered letters from friends who hoped to reach family members in the diaspora and began walking toward the Ivory Coast border. He carried his only possession, a bag, on his head Liberian style.

As expected, NPFL soldiers commanded by Charles Taylor guarded the border. A rebel soldier searched his bag and discovered the letters Olu was asked to carry. The rebels immediately turned hostile and accused Olu of being an accomplice working for the government of Samuel Doe.

They stripped him of his clothes and told him the penalty for his crime was death. Another Liberian had also been sentenced to die. Olu watched as the soldiers shot him without mercy. He did not know the young man's crime, but Olu was certain he had done nothing worthy of death. Just before Olu's execution, one of the commanders of the NPFL halted the proceedings. He looked at Olu and said, "Identify yourself! Why are you being interrogated?"

"My name is Olu Menjay. I have been arrested because in my bag they found letters I am carrying across the border to family members of my friends."

The commander repeated his name. "Menjay?"

"Yes."

"Are you related to Harrison Menjay?" asked the commander.

Olu was afraid to answer, realizing his response might determine whether he lived or died. Finally he said with fear, "Yes, I am just going to tell the truth here. He is my father."

"Where is your father?" the commander asked, sounding somewhat concerned.

Olu responded, "I don't know where he is. I haven't seen him for several months now."

In reply, the commander's tone of voice suddenly changed. "When I was a teenager in Nimba, I did not have enough money to go to school, but your father gave me a scholarship so I could go to the Baptist school." The commander gave orders for the men to give back Olu's clothes.

The same man who had given orders to execute anyone suspected of collaborating with the enemy was suddenly merciful. He gave Olu ten dollars and a hot Coke and told him he was allowed to cross the border.

As Olu dressed, he thought about his father and his father's good name, a name that had saved his life.

"That taught me what a good name can do for you," Olu says now. We read in Proverbs 22:1, "A good name is more desirable than great riches; to be esteemed is better than silver or gold" (NIV). This was certainly the case for Olu.

After crossing over into the Ivory Coast, Olu survived as a refugee by working on farms and doing relief work. During his time there, he remembered the missionary friends from the United States who had worked with his father as co-laborers in planting Baptist churches in Liberia, in particular Rev. John Mark Carpenter and his wife, Betty.

Eventually, Olu was able to call the Carpenters and tell them his plight. He also wrote them letters. They stayed in contact with one another while he lived as a refugee in the Ivory Coast. Rev. Carpenter knew Olu was a young man of promise and wanted to help him. He wrote a letter to his former college classmate, Dr. H. M. Fulbright, then-president of Truett-McConnell College, requesting that he grant Olu a scholarship, which he did.

After Olu was accepted at Truett-McConnell College, the next step was to get him back to Liberia, out of the country, and to the United States, which was no small task. School started at the college on January 5. As of December 28, 1990, Olu was still a refugee in the Ivory Coast.

Olu went to the United States Embassy in Abidjan, Ivory Coast, seeking a student visa. However, the consulate would not issue a visa unless Olu could produce a plane ticket from Liberia. Olu learned of a United Nations ship leaving from Abidjan bound for Monrovia. The ship was carrying more than 500 Liberians back to their homeland, so Olu boarded. The journey took three days and three nights. There was no food for the people aboard the vessel. Fortunately, Olu carried a little bread he hoped would sustain him.

The ship docked at Free Port Harbor in Monrovia on New Year's Eve. Olu was reunited with his parents for the first time since the civil war broke out. The reunion was joyful but painfully brief. He attended the traditional all-night New Year's Watch Night service at church with his family.

The next day he met Rev. Carpenter, who had flown to Monrovia for relief work and a building ministry. While there, he gave Olu money to purchase a plane ticket back to Abidjan, where Olu got his visa approved for the United States. From there, he purchased his ticket to America.

On January 2, 1991, Olu left the country where he had lived as a refugee of the Liberian civil war for nearly two years, just three days before he was to begin college in a country he had never seen.

He felt excitement in leaving but also profound sadness. His country was torn apart by civil war, with his family caught in the middle of it all. His father worked hard to minister and provide answers to a struggling Christian community. Olu was no longer a refugee exiled in a foreign country. He was leaving it behind. He knew he was one of the lucky ones.

As he left, his country was still in shambles. Liberia had lost much of her good name. Olu went away with great hope that one day he could return and help his country regain some of what she had lost.

Chapter 2

Sowing the Seeds of Conflict

The American Colonization Society and the Founding of Liberia

It's impossible to comprehend the destruction of hope as families were ripped apart and taken from their homeland in the American slave trade. To underscore their plight, African and African-American scholars sometimes call the slave trade "Maafa," meaning "holocaust" and affecting between nine and twelve million people.

After such events as the American Slave Trade, the Trail of Tears, and the Jewish Holocaust, we should always be aware of the danger that exists when people hold views of hatred or espouse claims of superiority over other groups. Such attitudes are slippery slopes to discrimination, marginalization, and domination, which can easily lead to a loss of basic human rights, persecution, and crushed hope and human dignity.

If we think such events are only in the rearview mirror of history, we ignore the sea of oppressed people of this world who are denied the right to an education, to earn a decent living wage, to own property, to vote, to receive health care, to worship any god or no god at all, to assemble, to enjoy a free press, to express themselves in free speech, and even to protect their bodies. When denied these basic rights, people are demeaned of value, and their hope is lost.

My trips to Liberia led me to study our country's connection with Liberia's birth and the causes of her recent civil war. I concluded that the American Slave Trade was the seedbed of the Liberian civil war. For the first time, I realized that the sins of people up to seven or more generations ago were handed down like a time bomb that exploded in twentieth-century Liberia with enough shrapnel to spread into the new millennium. We are so far removed from the days of slavery that we find it difficult to believe there could be a connection between a modern-day civil war in an African country and the slave-trading days in the United States, yet it is true.

Family systems theory teaches that members of a family cannot be understood in isolation from one another, but must be viewed in relation to the whole family system. A family system is more than one's immediate family. It includes the generations from which the family has come. Behaviors, beliefs, attitudes, professions, mannerisms, education levels, and more can be passed down to members of the next generation.

Those born into healthy family systems usually transition from one stage of life into another without major problems. Those from dysfunctional families tend to have dysfunctional issues in adulthood. Unless they develop a self-awareness of their problems and through counseling and/or good decision making move away from their dysfunctional lifestyle, the next generation is born into it, learns it, and is subject to repeat it. On a grander scale, this can happen in communities, societies, and even nations.

Consequences of the American Slave Trade

The slave trade left deep scars on both sides of the Atlantic. In America, the relationship between blacks and whites remained precarious for more than a century after slaves were freed. Each generation reaped the previous generation's attitude toward race relations. Progress has been slow.

Even after being freed, generations of blacks struggled for fair treatment and rights equal to those of whites. Blacks suffered great prejudice as they looked for jobs with fair wages, equal-opportunity education, equal access to public facilities, equal rights under the law, and, as important as anything, kindness and respect. It took a civil rights movement before American whites were ready to deal with past sins. It took hard work to create a country and society where equal rights are extended to all people without regard to skin color.

When the Pilgrims landed at Plymouth Rock in America, it didn't take them long to discover that the New World already had tenants. Relationships with Native Americans were cordial at first, but eventually turned sour. As more people came from England to settle the New World, the land of the Native American soon became the land of the white man. As years passed, less of the land was negotiated. More was taken. Nearly all of it eventually became the land of the white man. The Native American's fate ended with the Trail of Tears. The attitude was simply this: the white man believed he was superior to the Native American and used his advanced weapons to prove it. Likewise, slavery existed because the white man believed he was superior to the black man. He proved it with his ability to enslave him.

As emancipation from slavery began in the United States, whites came to believe the races could not coexist. Separation was essential. The Native Americans and the freed slaves would need to be excised: the Native Americans to reservations, the blacks to a colony.

In Africa, the freed slaves, as they began to settle into their new land, quickly developed a superior attitude toward the indigenous population. They learned this attitude of superiority from their former slave masters.

The Establishment of a Colony for Freed Slaves

As early as 1800, the Virginia Legislature began exploring the possibility of finding a place to send free Negroes who were "exercising a pernicious influence on the character of the slaves."[1] Thomas Jefferson opposed such a settlement in the confines of the United States but was open to the idea if territory could be found elsewhere. Jefferson was aware of a colony already established by the British in Sierra Leone. The Virginia Legislature turned their attention to the continent of Africa. Upon further inquiry, it was discovered that the British-run colony had nearly failed because of many obstacles and was no longer taking free slaves.

Independent of the work taking place in the Virginia Legislature, the idea of a colony attracted a minister—Dr. Robert Finley, pastor of the Presbyterian Church at Princeton University. Dr. Finley was an uncommonly successful preacher from New Jersey. Determined to find some benevolent cause that would make a huge impact on society, Finley developed a zealous plan to form a colonization society. At the Presbyterian Church in the borough of Princeton, he hosted a public meeting where he explained to a small group of professors at the college and theological seminary his hopes for colonizing the free people of color on the western coast of Africa.

Notable friends in attendance were Elias B. Caldwell and Francis Scott Key. They accompanied Finley to Washington, where a public meeting was held in order for Finley to present his plan to some of the District of Columbia's most distinguished men. The Honorable Henry Clay chaired the meeting. Of note is the speech made to the group by Elias Caldwell:

> We say in the Declaration of Independence, "that all men are created equal," and have certain "unalienable rights." Yet it is considered impossi-

ble, consistently with the safety of the State, and it is certainly impossible with the present feelings towards these people, that they can ever be placed upon this equality, or admitted to the enjoyment of these "inalienable rights" while they remain mixed with us. Some persons may declaim and call it prejudice. No matter. Prejudice is as powerful a motive, and will as certainly exclude them as the soundest reason. Others may say they are free enough. If this is a matter of opinion let them judge—if of reason, let it be decided by our repeated and solemn declarations in all our public acts. This state of society unquestionably tends, in various ways, to injure the morals and destroy the habits of industry among our people. This will be acknowledged by every person who has paid any attention to the subject, and it seems to be so generally admitted that it would promote the happiness of the people, and the interest of the people, to provide a place where these people might be settled by themselves, that it is unnecessary to dwell on this branch of the subject.[2]

Caldwell makes it clear that certain words of the Declaration of Independence—"that all men are created equal" and that all have "unalienable rights"—could never apply to the freed slave. He believed it was impossible and that hope for both races lay with a colonization effort in Africa. If freed slaves remained among whites, he did not see hope for harmonious living.

Caldwell argued that if freed slaves stayed in America, they would expect education. Yet even if they were to attain some skill, they would not be allowed to use it in the current society. So any skills they acquired, any knowledge they gained, would in the end not benefit them, but harm them because it would make them more miserable since they would be unable to put it to use. To leave them in America, argued Caldwell, was nothing more than false hope.

Caldwell's reasoning almost sounds noble. In trying to make the wrongs of slavery right, these men could not imagine a day when men and women who were once bought and sold like animals might live equal to them in any way. They desired liberty and freedom for the former slaves, but not where they would share the same rights, not where they would meet on the street and do business with the same families who once owned them and called them slaves. Perhaps these men simply could not face a constant reminder of their sin. It was easier to send the freed people away.

The committee drew up a resolution to create the American Society for Colonizing the Free People of the United States to present to the House of Representatives. This resolution asked for the aid of the general government to establish a territory to colonize free people of color in Africa or elsewhere, but not in the United States. By the time a vote was held in December 1816, the idea had gained momentum. When the bill came to the floor for a vote, only nine voters dissented in the House and one in the Senate. In January 1817, the American Colonization Society was formed in the city of Washington, D.C.

Full emancipation of slaves would not occur until the end of the Civil War. The American Colonization Society dealt with the problem of slaves who had won their freedom or escaped to freedom. Those who established the American Colonization Society believed they had found a viable solution to the problem posed by the growing number of freed slaves. They believed both whites and blacks would receive the idea well. They believed they were helping repair a great evil in America by aiding the freed slaves in their "pursuit of happiness and independence which a benign Providence had left open to the human race."

The new society received support from a number of different groups for many reasons. Slave owners supported it because freed slaves were one of the greatest sources of insecurity and loss of profit to the slaveholder. Freed slaves gave encouragement to other slaves that they, too, might attain their freedom. Runaway slaves resulted in a great loss of income for slaveholders, especially plantation holders who needed large numbers of slaves to harvest crops. Abolitionists viewed the practice of slavery as immoral and inhumane.

In reality, the efforts of the society were a grasp in the dark for something that might ease the tension between whites and freed slaves without addressing the problem directly. Officially, the importation of slaves was banned by Congress and signed into law by Thomas Jefferson in 1807, going into effect on January 1, 1808. However, the law did not stop the buying and selling of slaves. Even as money was raised and freed slaves were prepared to board ships for the coast of West Africa, the law prohibiting new slaves from arriving on the shores of the United States was poorly enforced. Mostly, the law drove the slave trade underground. Illegal ships continued to arrive from Africa to feed the continued demand of Southern plantation cotton growers even as ships crossed the Atlantic to carry freed slaves back to Africa.

There is no record that a representative from the freed blacks was consulted regarding how his people felt about the creation of a colony for them in West Africa. Perhaps the Virginia Legislature believed the freed slaves would be grateful considering the alternative. Black leaders initially rejected the plans of the American Colonization Society. "They protested eloquently that they had been born in America and considered themselves Americans. In many cases their fathers had fought and shed blood for American freedom. They felt no connection to Africa, and sought none. Their focus was on political recognition by the majority in the North and abolition of slavery in the South. They rightly recognized colonization as a movement that would sap strength from the sympathetic portion of the white population, while indirectly thwarting their aims by spreading the propaganda of black inferiority."[3]

The American Colonization Society alienated most of the people they needed to make their vision grow by describing African Americans as a vicious and degraded race. Even so, they found enough freed slaves to keep the boats full with prospective new African immigrants.

The society was a mixed bag of hope. It offered hope to slaves who had little or no hope for beginning a new and meaningful life in the racially charged environment where they lived. It offered hope to whites who believed their quality of life would improve once the freed slaves were colonized.

Almost two centuries later, we can easily surmise that racial cleansing was the society's main goal. We can recognize deep prejudices even among the most God-fearing people. Just because it had its beginnings in a church didn't make it Christian. The freed slaves who boarded ships for West Africa did so with hope, however misguided. They could never know that this hope, which grew from a crooked branch, would be passed down and have devastating effects on their African-born descendants.

The Crooked Branch

John O'Sullivan, an influential advocate for the Democratic Party in the 1830s, championed the idea that it was America's God-given destiny to reach out and claim territory in order to spread America's principles and values into other countries of the world. God (Providence) had given America a mission to spread democracy throughout the world. This was God's manifest. This was America's destiny. The doctrine of Manifest Destiny used the Christian influence within the American Colonization Society to establish that America had a divine right to expand over the continent and establish a colony for freed slaves in West Africa. While the real reason for establishing the colony was to purge America of freed slaves, many people insisted that this venture was sanctioned from "on high."

The ideal carried into Liberia was built on John Winthrop's Puritan concept of a "City on the Hill," a new Jerusalem founded in God's honor. Winthrop believed the Puritans had formed a special agreement with God and were God's chosen ones, the "people of Israel." The freed slaves went to Liberia with this attitude. They were told that they were God's chosen ones, chosen to take the land, chosen to integrate the darkness of Africa with the Christian faith.

The feeling of entitlement regarding the land set the stage for poor relationships with the indigenous people. The newcomers from America conveyed their understanding of providential guidance by naming the island near the mouth of the Mesurado River where they first settled "Providence Island." Established by freed slaves, the first Baptist church, which is on one of the highest points in the city of Monrovia, was named Providence Baptist Church.

On the surface, the African immigrants' hope seemed to grow despite the hardships caused by disease and the struggle of adjusting to a new environment. However, an enemy of hope was sown from the time the Americo-Liberians landed on the shores of Western Africa. The freed slaves were oblivious to the damage they were doing to the indigenous people in the land they claimed as their own. This shaky relationship ultimately broke the back of the country and thrust the people into a civil war 169 years after the *Elizabeth*, a ship carrying freed slaves, docked off the coast of modern-day Liberia.

Notes

1. Alexander Archibald, *A History of Colonization on the Western Coast of Africa* (Philadelphia: W. S. Martien, 1846) 62.

2. Ibid., 82–83.

3. Douglas Harper, "American Colonization Society," in *Slavery in the North* (2003), http://www.slavenorth.com/colonize.htm.

Chapter 3

Strangers in a Strange Land

An American Education

Olu arrived in Chicago on Saturday, January 5, 1991, wearing short sleeves and carrying no luggage. Following a seven-hour layover, he flew to Atlanta. Admission counselor Rev. Wayne Wilkes from Truett-McConnell College picked him up at 10:00 p.m. and drove him to his new home in Cleveland, Georgia.

After only a few hours' sleep, Olu awoke and was ready to leave for church when Dr. David Hinson, the pastor of Cleveland First Baptist Church, arrived.

Olu still remembers Dr. Hinson's bright red pickup truck and his warm, friendly smile. In the short three and a half miles to church, a friendship developed that has had a deep and lasting effect on Olu's life.

Following the worship service, Dr. Hinson introduced Olu to American culture with a trip to Wal-Mart, where they purchased supplies for college: clothing, bedding, soap, an iron, and the typical items any student needs to begin life in a college dorm. After one shopping experience at Wal-Mart, Olu had more possessions than he'd owned in several years.

Though it wasn't easy, over the next two years, Olu adjusted to his new home in America in a dorm at Truett-McConnell College. He was excited to be back in school, and the environment challenged him academically. Olu also enjoyed plenty of food and saw more things to eat in the cafeteria than he'd ever seen in Liberia or the Ivory Coast except in the marketplaces.

In Liberia and as a refugee, Olu ate rice every day and enjoyed greens occasionally. Not long after he arrived at Truett-McConnell College, a teacher discovered that Olu missed these foods and decided to prepare them for him. Olu was invited to the teacher's home for a meal.

As Olu sat at the table, he noticed the bowl of huge leaves. The collard greens looked nothing like the finely chopped spiced cassava he was used to eating in Liberia.[1] It was clear that "greens" in Liberia and "greens" in America were not the same. He politely managed to chew up a few bites of the collards and enjoyed lots of rice.

In addition to adjusting to the food, Olu had to adjust to his new environment. He met many friendly people at school, but he often felt lonely in this strange country. He also felt guilty for leaving his family behind in Liberia. He knew that his most important task was his academic pursuit, so he immersed himself in his studies. He also worked hard on campus to earn spending money, serving in the cafeteria and in the maintenance department and sending as much of his salary as possible back to his family in Liberia.

Cassava is being cut into small pieces and pounded in a messa. Peppers will be added and this will be cooked over a fire for a fine Liberian meal.

Olu graduated from Truett-McConnell College in June 1993 at the top of his class. He then faced a decision: what should he do next? He felt torn between working to support his family in Liberia or continuing his education. Olu considered Shorter College. Dr. Hinson suggested Mercer University, but Olu thought the $15,000 per year price tag was far too high. Dr. Hinson gave him life-changing advice, telling Olu not to allow money to stop him from following God's wishes for his life. He said, "If you become convinced God wants you to do something, you must believe in God."

Dr. Hinson wrote a letter to Dr. Kirby Godsey, then-president of Mercer University, and told him Olu's story. Like Dr. Fulbright at Truett-McConnell College, Dr. Godsey made it possible for Olu to attend Mercer.

As a Mercer student in summer 1993, Olu was hired as a summer missionary at Camp Kaleo, a Royal Ambassador camp in Forsyth, Georgia, owned and operated by the Georgia Baptist Convention. The concept of summer camp was not foreign to him, since he had participated in Royal Ambassador (R.A.) camps in Liberia prior to the civil war. Although most Americans think they're roughing it at Camp Kaleo, Olu was overwhelmed by the facilities—nice cabins, a ropes course, gymnasium, pool, cafeteria, forty-acre lake where campers canoe and fish, outdoor worship center, and miles of trails through beautiful South Georgia woods.

The summer offered a great opportunity for Olu to work with a staff of peers and participate in the planning and programming of a well-run camp led by director Brad Smith. Olu expanded his small but growing network of Baptist friends in Georgia. At Camp Kaleo, Olu had his first real chance to serve with young people since arriving from Liberia.

Olu felt that he was on the receiving end of God's grace. He was ready to give, and Camp Kaleo offered him that opportunity. It became an important stepping stone in Olu's decision to move toward vocational ministry.

This was a natural path for him. The Royal Ambassador program in Liberia played a significant role in shaping Olu into a young leader. As a teenager, he had been elected as the vice president of the Royal Ambassador program for the country of Liberia.[2]

At Camp Kaleo, Olu stood out among the all-white staff and mostly white campers. Whenever he spoke, the boys paid close attention to his Liberian accent. Olu's testimony was compelling, not only for the campers, but for his fellow staffers. He caused people to stop and give thanks for what they took for granted.

I was invited to be camp pastor for a week that summer when Olu served as a missionary at Camp Kaleo. During the week, Olu and I had an opportunity for our relationship to grow, and my interest in his life and the plight of his people increased. Knowing him helped me understand the blessings of health, food, family, freedom, and material things. I wondered what the future held for Olu and his people.

The summer at Camp Kaleo continued Olu's development of his calling into ministry. He had entered Mercer with a desire to work in public policy. He left the university with a calling on his life to enter ministry. After his graduation from Mercer, Olu was accepted as a seminary student at Duke Divinity School.

The Letter I Almost Threw Away

During Olu's first year of seminary studies at Duke, I went to the post office one day in Clarkesville and discovered a letter in the box with a return address from Liberia. With great curiosity, I opened the letter. It read,

Dear Dr. Helms:

We bring you greetings in the matchless name of our Savior and Lord Jesus
Christ. It is our honor, through Bro. Olu Menjay, to introduce what may
seem foreign, but Christ centered. YouthChallenge Liberia is a nationwide
Youth Ministry Consortium that is uniquely Liberian, distinctly Christian
and definitely relevant in postwar Liberia by providing training, resources
and encouragement to youth and youth workers around the country.

    With all these aspirations, Bro. Menjay has forwarded me your name
as one of the qualified pastors who may serve as the keynote speaker for
our coming event. We are honored to invite you as the keynote speaker at
our second pastor's consultation lecture on Youth Ministry on Friday,
December 15, 1995, at the Fourth National Youth Workers Development
Workshop . . . .

    In the case of any details or further questions, please contact Bro.
Menjay at the below address.

    . . . We look forward to your response as YouthChallenge becomes a
challenge to our challenging world of youth in Liberia.

    Goodbye for now and God blessing.

In His Service,
Rev. Caleb S. G. Dormah
National Director
YouthChallenge, Liberia

It wasn't exactly an invitation to Disney World. Most pastors are vain
enough to fantasize about being invited to speak in the great pulpits or serve
as a speaker in demand for revivals and other events. I had been asked to
help with several Disciple Now weekends, and I looked forward to being the
camp pastor at Camp Kaleo each summer for several years. Even so, I wasn't
a speaker in demand. Even if I were, I would have put Liberia at the bottom
of the list of places from which I hoped to receive an invitation.

    Everything I knew about Liberia I had learned from Olu, and I didn't
particularly want to see anything there. What stuck in my mind was that a
person could get killed there, and I wasn't keen on martyrdom.

    I was tempted to throw the letter away, but I kept it for a while in my
desk and eventually called Olu to ask him about Caleb. I expected Olu to
give me a Liberian laugh and say something like, "Caleb should know better
than to invite you to Liberia. He ought to know you can't consider going to
Liberia at a time like this. That man's got to be crazy, Michael."

Six years earlier, the rebel commander had spared Olu's life and allowed him to cross the border into Ivory Coast. Olu had returned to Liberia only briefly to get money from Reverend Carpenter so he could buy a ticket out of the country. Going to Liberia wasn't a high priority for anyone. Getting out was. Even Reverend Carpenter was cautious about the timing of his trips.

I waited for Olu to give me permission to wad up the letter and throw it in the trash, but he never did. Instead, he allowed me to struggle with the invitation. He actually asked me once if I would go. After all, he had given Caleb my name. He sensed something in me; I'm not sure what.

Caleb's letter lacked the drama of a vision like the Apostle Paul received one night from Macedonian man who stood and begged him to come over and help them (Acts 16:9). Even so, the letter had the same effect on me. Here was a man in another country saying, "We need hope over here. Will you please come and share with us what you know about leading youth to Jesus?"

Many times invitations or dreams seem impossible, so we entertain such thoughts only briefly. We forget that God has worked in the impossibility department for a long time. I remembered the concept Dr. Hinson taught Olu: "If you become convinced God wants you to do something, you must believe in God." I wasn't yet convinced that God wanted me to go to Liberia, but by keeping the letter I acknowledged that God might have a reason for allowing it to end up in my mailbox.

As I began to think of all the reasons I should not go, God showed me how he goes before us and prepares the way. I mentioned the invitation to travel to Liberia to some of the leaders in my church. *That ought to put a stop to it,* I thought. *These folks will let me know quickly that my focus should be on my job right here with them and that I don't have any business going across the Atlantic to lead a youth conference.* Instead, I discovered that three members of Clarkesville Baptist had already traveled to Liberia.

During the 1980s, the Georgia Baptist Convention formed a partnership with the Liberia Baptist Missionary and Educational Convention. Hundreds of Georgians traveled to Liberia during that decade to assist in a wide range of projects. In my church, Hal Sisk went to help build a bridge. Julian Gissendanner went to help dig a well. Wink Hicks, former Women's Missionary Union president for Georgia Baptists, went to work with the Baptist Women of Liberia. Liberia wasn't exactly a paradise in the 1980s, either. My friends' travels occurred under the regime of Samuel Doe, who had assassinated President (and Baptist minister) William Tolbert.

Uh-oh. I don't usually use coincidence and God in the same sentence. Neither do I look for God behind every rock and bush, but I didn't want God to have to hit me in the head with a two-by-four plank to get my attention. God had sent me to a church that was truly excited about Liberia, loved Liberia, and embraced the possibility of my traveling to Liberia. The people were aware that the country's situation had deteriorated since Georgia Baptists had traveled there. My safety was their only concern. They began to pray with me that God would make his will clear regarding the trip.

In 1995, when I received Caleb's invitation, Liberia was a dangerous place. The country was overrun with ex-combatants and criminals. It was a place of little law and even less justice. Although the United Nations had a peacekeeping presence in Monrovia, peace was fragile. A travel advisory was in effect for foreigners.

The primary airport, Roberts International, was closed. Runways were damaged during the fighting and thus unusable. Only a small landing strip in Monrovia allowed planes into the country. Two flights a week went into and out of Monrovia from Sierra Leone, meaning that only about thirty people per week entered or left this nation of about two and a half million people. The country was practically isolated from the outside world, cut off by fighting and unrest.

I decided the only wise and feasible way to make such a trip was to travel with Olu. After much prayer, I told Olu that if he would accompany me to Liberia, I would go. The kind and generous members of Clarkesville Baptist would pay for our trip.

I had traveled to a third-world country only once before, when I went to Jamaica, famous for its tourist attractions like Ocho Rios and Montego Bay. However, I spent my time in Kingston. Few tourists travel to Kingston, a city with a depressed economy and the highest murder rate in the world. Although our group stayed in nice quarters across the street from the University of the West Indies, my time in Jamaica was enough of an immersion into a third-world culture that I experienced the typical shock of seeing it for the first time. However, even that trip didn't fully prepare me for Liberia.

Every reason not to go to Liberia related to my safety, my family, and my comfort level. When asked why I was going, my only answer was that I had been invited and I believed God would bless the trip.

As I prepared to leave, my mind wandered back to my college days at Samford University. One evening I attended a worship service at Dawson

Memorial Baptist Church. A missionary from Africa, a physician, gave a presentation on his work. More than twenty-five years later, I cannot remember much about that service, but I recall that at the end, I felt moved to respond to the invitation. I went forward, but several people already were speaking to the counselors. I left.

My heart had been stirred that night for the people in a foreign land. I admired the work the missionaries did. As a boy, I was taught well by R.A. leaders in my church. As an older teenager, I worked with my future father-in-law, who led a group of Royal Ambassadors on Saturday mornings. Mr. Haywood instilled in those boys the importance of missions and sharing the love of Christ both with people around us and with people in other countries.

I made a commitment to ministry as an eleven-year-old, announcing to my church that God had called me to be a preacher. As a high school senior, I reaffirmed that call. My church licensed me to the gospel ministry, and soon thereafter a church in the county called me as their pastor. I remained there for two years until I transferred from Troy State University to Samford University.

I was already committed to continuing my education in seminary. I wasn't responding to the invitation that night in order to commit my life to foreign missions. I suppose it was more of an affirmation of Isaiah 6:8: "Then I heard the voice of the Lord saying, 'Whom shall I send? And who will go for us?' And I said, 'Here am I. Send me!'"

I had that attitude as Olu and I met at Hartsfield International Airport in Atlanta, Georgia, on a December evening, two weeks before Christmas in 1995, for a trip that proved to be life-changing for both of us. In September, when I first received Caleb's invitation to Liberia, I never thought I'd actually go. When I found myself ready to travel, I thought the trip was about what God wanted to do with *me*, what God wanted to teach and show *me*. Why shouldn't I have thought that? The letter was addressed to me. *I* was the one invited to teach.

Perhaps God was fulfilling Isaiah 6:8 in my life. He was sending me to the mission field for a brief time. However, the trip to Liberia wasn't really about *me*. It had to do with what God was going to do in Olu's life and in the lives he would touch in the years to come. God used me as a catalyst for Olu's future work in Liberia.

When we are obedient to God's guidance, we are not always given a clear reason for his leading. Sometimes, it takes weeks, months, or years before we are able to look back and see how God's plan unfolded in our lives. We may need the perspective of heaven before we know the reasons for many of the things we are asked to do.

While the trip certainly changed my life, it set the course for Olu's life and ministry to his people in Liberia. The letter I almost threw away became the catalyst that opened the door for Olu's ministry in Liberia.

If I had thrown away that letter without a second thought, I know God would have found another way to get Olu to Liberia to begin a process of helping his people. However, I would have missed the blessings had I not been open to God's leading. I am grateful I had a front-row seat to witness God's work of bringing hope to the people in Liberia through Olu and Ricks Institute.

Notes

1. In Monrovia, farmers bring their produce to the city to sell, much like a farmers' market in America. There one can buy all kinds of things from vegetables to meat. For example, one item easily available at the market is cassava, a staple in Liberia. The root resembles that of a turnip, and one can eat it raw or boiled. It can also be cut into small pieces, dried in the sun, and pounded into a fine powder. When water is added, it makes a high-starch food for babies. The bush of the plant grows several feet tall, and the leaves are harvested, chopped, and pounded finely in a messa. A messa is a two-piece wooden tool used as an important part in the preparation of food for cooking. The base is made from a hollowed out log and the "wand" which resembles a club is also made from parts of a tree. The wand is used to pound fruits and vegetables, separating the edible parts from the non-edible parts, and preparing foods for the cooking process. Liberians cook these greens over a fire, adding peppers for flavor. It results in a tasty dish.

2. The Royal Ambassador program is one of the most successful programs Baptist missionaries implemented in Liberia. The program trained thousands of boys to do their best to become well-informed followers of Christ, to have Christlike concern for all people, and to keep themselves clean and healthy in mind and body.

Chapter 4

Taking Root
The Price of Misplaced Hope

The *Elizabeth*

In every conflict, there are deep-seated reasons why people choose to take up arms against one another. As the American Colonization Society carried freed slaves to West Africa, the freed people arrived with a belief system influenced by the religion and values of their former masters that put them on an immediate collision course with the indigenous population.

As the sun rose on Sierra Leone on March 10, 1820, a ship sat in the harbor filled with hopeful immigrants. Sierra Leone was not their final destination, but the eighty-eight black immigrants and three white company officials of the American Colonization Society aboard the *Elizabeth* had reached the continent of Africa.

The oldest among these hopeful souls was Nace Butler, a sixty-six-year-old carpenter from Washington, D.C.; the youngest was one-year-old Henrietta Cain, the child of Henry and Charlotte Cain of Philadelphia.

Regardless of their ages, the regions of America where they once lived, or how they had attained their freedom, the freed slaves shared a hope for a better tomorrow that had grown with each passing day aboard the *Elizabeth*. As they glimpsed the land from which their ancestors were taken, their hope surged.

The two-week voyage aboard the *Elizabeth* to Sierra Leone was a stark contrast to the voyages their ancestors had taken aboard slave ships such as the *Brookes, Cora, Pons, Triton, Wildfire*, and, ironically, *Hope*. There was no hope in the bows of such ships. They transported human cargo with less dignity than most people transport livestock. The numbers of slaves depended on the kind of ship, but in every ship, human beings were stacked on top of one another like cords of wood. Some ships carried more than 800 slaves.

In 1829, the Reverend Robert Walsh went aboard the slave ship *Feloz*, a broad-decked ship with a mainmast, schooner rigged, which had a formidable gun behind her foremast. On board he found 336 males and 226 females—562 slaves. These slaves had been aboard the ship for seventeen days, during which time fifty-five had died and were thrown overboard. Walsh found that all the slaves were "enclosed under grated hatchways between decks where space was so low that they sat between each other's legs and were stowed so close together that there was no possibility of their lying down or at all changing their position by night or day."[1]

Most striking to Walsh was how it was possible for such a large number of human beings to be packed and wedged together in low cells three feet high, the greater part of which was shut off from light or air, running the temperature near 90 degrees. The heat of these horrid places was so great and the odor so offensive that it was impossible for an outsider to enter. Walsh remembered that many of the survivors were seen lying about the decks in the last stage of emaciation and in a state of filth and misery. In addition, the effects of disease were not lost on the crew of the ship either, as eight or nine had died and six more lay in hammocks in different stages of fever.[2] The amount of suffering aboard the slave ships brought out deep laments from the African slaves as they traveled toward American shores. Their cries fell on the uncompassionate ears of their transporters.

Contrast the journeys of the hopeless slaves aboard the slave ships with the journey of the freed slaves aboard the *Elizabeth*. The mood must have grown more festive with each passing day as they drew closer to a promised land where they would be free of the slave master's call to duty, free to speak their minds, free to assemble, and free to choose their own paths in life.

Looking at the starry sky above, perhaps Nace Butler, the senior statesman aboard the *Elizabeth,* pointed to the Big Dipper and the North Star and reminded the immigrants that those constellations were used as navigation points to help some of them make their escape to freedom through the Underground Railroad. Such stories of hope would be passed down from generation to generation, keeping hope alive and helping hope grow for future generations.

As they sat in the harbor at Sierra Leone, waiting to sail down the coast to their eventual landing site, these hopeful souls believed they were going to have rich stories to tell their grandchildren about being the first group to arrive in the new land aboard the *Elizabeth*.

Just as the Jews exiled in Babylon discovered that God was with them in a foreign land, the slaves had discovered that God was with them in the cotton fields of the Deep South and in other regions of the country. They brought that faith with them to their new land that was later named Liberia, which means "the country of the free." God had not forsaken them through their time of slavery. As they returned to the home of their ancestors, they believed God was still with them, and their hope grew.

While the West African coastline with its tranquil waters, lush jungle, fertile soil, and trees that carried food year-round looked inviting to those aboard the *Elizabeth,* they soon discovered a dark side to the warmth and pristine surroundings. West Africa's warm climate and stagnant pools of water result in a prime breeding ground for mosquitoes. The rainy season lasts six months, giving mosquitoes carrying diseases such as malaria and Yellow Fever opportunities to reproduce without interference.[1]

As the *Elizabeth* settled in the waters just off the coast of modern-day Liberia, Yellow Fever soon began to find its way through the population. Within the first few weeks after arriving, 14 percent of those aboard the *Elizabeth* had died from the disease. Among them were Henrietta Cain and her parents, Henry and Charlotte. Another 10 percent died within the next four years from the fever or other maladies. Among those was Nace Butler, who drowned. Hope was growing at a high price.

Slavery, the Gospel, and Hope

The freed slaves hoped for a better quality of life, the opportunity to own property, the chance to govern themselves, and the ability to work for themselves and not for a white master or boss. They looked for freedoms: freedom of religion, freedom of speech, freedom of expression and self-determination. One can hardly blame them for striking out to give this grand experiment a try. However, it wasn't their attitudes, at least not in the initial stages of this grand experiment, that drove the exodus. Rather, it was the determination by whites that blacks and whites could not coexist in the States. Had attitudes been different in America, the freed slaves would never have desired to return to Africa. Once freed in a world dominated by whites, though, they found it nearly impossible to earn a living and to live without being harassed or unfairly treated.

It's obvious that, more than the Bible or church, society and culture were dominant factors that determined people's position on slavery. Slavery was a matter of economics. As history shows, many in the North began to oppose slavery, not because the people of the North were more Christian or morally superior to people of the South, but because slavery was not as economically profitable in the northern states. In fact, with factory-based economies, it was more economical to pay blacks a low wage than to own them. In the South, however, large numbers of slaves were necessary to harvest the cotton crops and run the large plantations, so owning them remained a high priority.

It's worth noting that the Southern Baptist Convention was born out of a conflict over how to do missions in the North and the South. The issue finally came to a head with the unwillingness of the Acting Board in Boston to appoint a slaveholder as a missionary. As a reaction, the Southern Baptist Convention was formed in Augusta in 1845. To put it bluntly, economics drove the theology of Southern Baptists on the issue of slavery. The need for slaves to keep the plantations open and the economy moving blinded Southerners to a Christ-centered interpretation of Scripture regarding slavery. In fact, coming to a Christ-centered interpretation of Scripture would have meant the end of the practice of slavery.

When the northern Baptists blocked the southern Baptists from sending missionaries, the southern Baptists formed their own group. Obviously, if Southerners were not willing to listen to the viewpoints of Northerners on the slavery issues, they cared nothing about the viewpoint of the slaves. While that point is obvious, it's important to say that the viewpoints of the oppressed are important. Such people have a unique perspective on Scripture. Their application of Scripture is usually different.

Instead of merely taking the gospel to the oppressed and explaining what it means, we need to allow the oppressed to teach us how they hear the gospel. Allowing them to tell us what it means to them, and what hope the Scripture brings to them, will open our eyes and ears to new understandings and applications of the gospel. If we walk among the oppressed and preach as if we have all the answers, always telling them to hold out their cups so we can pour in what we have, how can hope grow in us? How can the oppressed ever know that they have a place in God's kingdom? How will they know that God "chose things the world considers foolish in order to shame those who think they are wise"? We must remember that "God chose things that are powerless to shame those who are powerful. God chose things despised by the world, things counted as nothing at all, and used them to bring to nothing what the world considers important. As a result, no one can ever boast in the presence of God" (1 Cor 1:27-29, NLT).

Part of bringing hope to the oppressed is helping those individuals understand that they have something to offer the community of faith. Part of the value of listening to those who struggle greatly but still cling to hope is that we are often deeply inspired.

Looking back and seeing Christians' error on the issue of slavery is an important reminder that hope is not virtuous unless we hope for the things that are of God, blessed by God, and promote the will of God. People get caught up in false hope every day because of the fervor of the moment, because of the charisma of a great leader, because it seems to be the right thing to do, or because it is the direction the crowd is going. This kind of hope can start wars; suppress the rights of minorities, the weak, and the poor; and create cults. Nations and great leaders alike have fallen because of misplaced hope. Many have paid a huge price for daring to warn others of impending disaster because of misplaced hope.

Such misguided hope existed within the theology and philosophy of the slave masters and the American Colonization Society. They passed it down to the freed slaves. This misguided hope spread from one generation of Americo-Liberians (the descendants of freed slaves) to the next. It became more deadly than Yellow Fever, helping to create a culture that eventually erupted in a fourteen-year civil war.

Notes

1. "Aboard a Slave Ship, 1829," EyeWitness to History, www.eyewitnesstohistory.com (2000).

2. Ibid.

3. Once someone is bitten by a mosquito carrying the Yellow Fever, the virus remains dormant briefly in the body with an incubation period of three to six days. Fever, muscle pain, headaches, shivers, and loss of appetite, nausea, or vomiting usually follow. Most patients improve after three or four days, but in about 15 percent of the patients the fever enters a toxic phase, which kills within two weeks.

Chapter 5

Do You Really Believe this Gospel?

As Olu and I descended into Monrovia, our plane turned sharply, giving us a beautiful look at the beach below. From the air, it looked like paradise. That image was short lived.

As the plane touched down in Monrovia, I was shocked to see children running up and down the runway, waving as the plane taxied toward the terminal. Actually, "shed" is a better word to describe the building. There was no terminal—only a tin-roofed building for passengers to funnel through, getting passports stamped and arguing over who would check their luggage.

Hundreds of people gathered at the airport. They were loud. It was a chaotic and confusing scene. With such a small plane, I wondered why so many people waited at the airport. There were no celebrities on the plane, and I knew they were not waiting for us.

I discovered that these people gathered for the mere chance that they might see someone they recognized or someone who might have compassion and give them something of value—a belt, a watch, money, anything. Others hoped to carry a bag for a passenger and earn a small tip. The poor crowded at the airport because they knew if we had enough money to fly, then we should have money left in our pockets when we landed. These people were desperate. They hoped this would be their lucky day.

As a white traveler coming into the country, I was immediately a target of intrigue. Virtually no Americans or Europeans traveled to Liberia in 1995. At that time, Southern Baptists still had a missionary presence, but most missionary agencies had pulled their missionaries off the field, and Southern Baptists would soon follow.

People with authority at the airport sought to use their position to make money. As my bags came off the plane, they immediately caused an issue. Those who arrived to pick us up eventually escorted me to a waiting car while Olu and these men negotiated for my bags. This was a courteous gesture on their part. I soon discovered that a Liberian negotiating with a Liberian gained better results than a culture-shocked white American negotiating with a Liberian. My escorts also took my passport to get the necessary stamps so I wouldn't have to deal with the attention, although not having my passport made me uneasy.

As I waited that Sunday morning, I studied the car and my surroundings. At that time, most cars in Liberia looked like an American taxi that a dozen people beat with baseball bats. Huge potholes left from mortar fire during the civil war and the torrential rainfall of the rainy season (usually about 200 inches over the six-month season) pound the cars. Parts are nearly impossible to find, and damage simply becomes a permanent part of each car.

When my friends arrived with my luggage and passport, we all piled into the car Liberian style, which means it held twice as many people as it would carry in the States, and we headed to the church. As I looked at my watch, I noticed it was past time for the worship service to start. It occurred to me that the service might have already concluded, and the people would have gone home. Perhaps my preaching burden was lifted. Back home,

everybody would leave and go home if the visiting preacher was fifteen minutes late, much less three hours. I assumed that would be the case in Liberia, but my friends assured me the congregation would still be there.

The ride to the church unnerved me. I had little time to process the culture. The extent of the poverty, the smell of sewage flowing across city streets, the people without transportation forced to walk along the road, and the vast numbers of children who worked the streets hoping to sell something of value overwhelmed me.

As we turned onto the street where the church was located, a sea of people parted to allow our car to pass. When we pulled in front of

Olu Menjay sits in his father's office after worship at Second Providence Baptist Church in 1995, after being welcomed home for the first time since fleeing the violence of civil war.

Rev. Harrison J. Menjay, father, educator, and pastor.

the church, our car was the only one there. However, people were everywhere on this busy city street. Two boys dressed in Royal Ambassador
uniforms stood in front of the church. It was my first sign of a true Southern
Baptist presence in Liberia.

My friends had been correct; three hours after the service was supposed
to begin, the people of the church were indeed still there, still waiting.
They waited for Olu, their pastor's son, to return home, and they waited to
worship.

As soon as we stepped into the church, the celebration began. It had
been four years since Rev. and Mrs. Menjay had seen their second-born son.
Olu was returning to them from the United States as a college graduate, the
first college graduate in his family, the first college graduate from his entire
village.

As I look back, I think Olu should have received the honor of speaking
to the church that day. Although called to ministry, he was not yet ordained
(that ceremony took place later before he left to return to America).
Nevertheless, he should have preached that afternoon, but they gave the
honor to me. Actually, it was a burden. Even as I write this, tears come to my
eyes as I think of that day and the gift those people gave me, what they
taught me about worship, what their worship said to me about their faith,
and what their faith imparted to me about how we should live.

After the church sang in typical African style, with the beating of the
drums and the entire church dancing and clapping, Olu's father, Rev.
Harrison Menjay, welcomed me to the pulpit. I sat beside their twenty-six-
year-old associate minister, Emmanuel Wlue. As it was the week before
Christmas, this young man's name preached a message all its own.
Emmanuel means "God with us." I'd seen enough in my first hour in Liberia
to wonder if Liberia wasn't a God-forsaken place. It had already crossed my
mind: "Had these people ever wondered the same thing? Was God really
with the Liberian people?" I was to learn a valuable lesson from the Liberian
people, one I knew but had never seen demonstrated quite so remarkably:
love and joy are not dependent upon circumstances.

As the congregation continued to sing, Emmanuel leaned over to me
and said, "Dr. Helms, thank you for bringing hope to us. You are the first
American to come to us since the beginning of the war."

Although Emmanuel had never traveled far from his place of birth, perhaps not even out of Liberia, he sensed the sacrifice and effort I'd made to

come to his country. To him, it meant things were getting better. To him, my presence represented hope.

How I wished my presence would suffice as a sermon. The burden of saying anything of worth felt like a mountain on my shoulders. I desperately wanted to bring the Liberians a message of hope, but I wasn't sure I knew how to do that.

In difficult times like the civil war these people experienced, I realize that hope can atrophy or die altogether. However, I also know that one drop of rain in a drought is enough to keep people hoping for the end of the drought. One victim found alive beneath the rubble of a collapsed building can renew hope of finding additional survivors. One unexpected meal to a starving man is enough to give him hope for food tomorrow. Without offering false hope, I needed to offer a message of hope.

That morning, as I waited to speak at Second Providence Baptist Church, Johnson Street, Monrovia, Liberia, I feared opening my mouth and saying something that would send the people home disappointed. I felt entirely out of place. Even worse, with my sermon in hand, I asked myself, "Do you really believe what you are about to preach? Does the gospel you proclaim work here? If someone were to rise from his or her seat and ask where to find this loving God in the midst of the death, hunger, and suffering, what would you say?"

While I sat there asking myself these questions, Rev. Menjay stood, introduced me, and welcomed me to his pulpit. I stood before a congregation of abused and tired people. Some had been chased from their homes. Some had been raped. Many had seen people murdered. Perhaps some had even killed others in defense of their families. All of them were hungry, and most didn't know the source of tomorrow's meal. Many of the children had stopped playing. They no longer attended school. They were forced to work to find food. What gospel could I bring them? What words could I offer that would change their plight? What could I say that would increase their hope or alleviate their suffering?

I knew that, God willing, in a few days I would return to my home in America, where I would find adequate food, shelter, water, and enough money to pay all my bills with more left over to waste. I had a home, a car, a bank account, a retirement fund, and insurance. Had I placed all my trust in these material comforts? Would I still praise God if it all disappeared?

I stood before a room full of Jobs, a room full of suffering people. How many of them had his faith? How many of them would say, "Though he slay me, yet will I hope in him . . ." (Job 13:15a, NIV)? Had you been in their church that day and heard the joyous way the people sang, you would know they still found hope in God.

I cannot recall the message I had prepared. I can tell you what I actually said. You might not even call it a sermon. I attempted to express to those people the incredible strength I saw in their faith. I wanted them to know that if my faith were tested like theirs, I hoped it would prove as genuine and strong. I told the congregation that many of them were happier and had more joy in their lives than many people in America.

The Apostle Paul's joy did not depend on circumstances, good or bad. He wrote to the church at Philippi: "I know what it is to be in need, and I know what it is to have plenty. I have learned the secret of being content in any and every situation, whether well fed or hungry, whether living in plenty or in want. I can do everything through him who gives me strength" (Phil 4:12-13, NIV).

I explained that in America, many people had lost sight of Paul's secret. Instead, they thought the secret to joy was having material possessions. Yet I knew many people with great wealth, several cars, more than one house, plenty of food, and lots of money, but little joy.

Two days before I left for my trip to Liberia, tragedy struck members of my congregation. I had received a phone call in the early morning hours from a member of my congregation. She told me a fire had destroyed her brother's home in Atlanta. It appeared that the three occupants in the home—her brother, her sister-in-law, and her niece—had all burned to death. The deceased man's mother was also a member of my church.

This family had dealt with other issues of grief and illness, but this was far deeper than anything they had ever faced. As I ministered to them throughout the next day, the news grew worse. This beautiful family with a gorgeous home in an upscale Atlanta neighborhood suffered issues far beyond what anyone imagined. A suicide note was found in the man's truck. As it turned out, the incident involved a double homicide, arson, and suicide.

I shared this story with the people of Second Providence Baptist in Liberia because I wanted them to know that even those with great wealth suffer. I wanted them to understand that while it is not bad to want and pray for material things—especially food, shelter, and clothing—joy comes from a deeper well, a well I was convinced many of them had discovered as the source of living water; otherwise, they would not continue to worship and praise God in the midst of such devastation.

My goal that morning was to affirm their faith, to applaud their faith, and to tell them that I didn't come as their teacher, but rather as a student to listen to the lessons they had learned as they walked through the valley of the shadow of death.

As I stood to preach that Sunday, my hope was strengthened by the gathering community of believers of Second Providence Baptist Church. I wish I could have transported every member of my church from Clarkesville to the sanctuary that day. In spite of all their suffering, hardships, grief, and uncertainty, the joy of the Lord was the strength of the people of Second Providence Baptist Church. Their joy was evident in their songs, in their greeting, in their praise, and in their pastor, Rev. Harrison Menjay. These people were a people of hope. God was with them.

When I finished the sermon, Rev. Menjay came to me, shook my hand, and said to me, "Thank you for bringing to us the 'thus saith the Lord.'" I have never forgotten his words. I've often prayed that God would speak through me. Never have I felt like I needed God's help more than I needed it that day.

A smattering of amens around the church supported Rev. Menjay's words, led by the deacons who sat together to my right and the choir who sat to my left. There was young Emmanuel behind me who had first encouraged me and said my presence brought hope to the people. There was the congregation before me extending their warm farewells as we prepared to exit the church.

It was the most humbling worship experience of my life. I had never felt more unworthy to bring the gospel. Tears welled in my eyes. When I began, I wondered if I even believed what I was about to say. When I finished the message, I knew I believed it because the very people who asked me to come bring hope to them had renewed hope in me.

Chapter 6

Bearing Bad Fruit
Conflict Erupts between Newcomers and Indigenous People

Relating with Native Tribesmen

From the beginning, the native West African tribesmen regarded the new-comers, those freed slaves from America, with suspicion. The apprehension intensified as the immigrants increased in number, acquired more land, cut forests, killed game, interfered with the slave trade, and sought to impose the Christian religion upon the natives. Relations were further strained by the attitude of superiority manifested by blacks from America. The immigrants referred contemptuously to the natives as "savages and heathens."

John Hartwell Cocke, a general in the War of 1812, a member of the Virginia Legislature from 1831–1832, and a member of the American Colonization Society, received a letter from his former slave Peyton Skipworth in 1834, sixteen years after the first immigrants settled in Liberia. The letter (printed in original form) not only shows the freed slaves' attitude toward indigenous people, but also demonstrates the pecking order that soon developed between the two groups:

> Dear Sir: I embrace this oppertunity to inform you that we are all in mod-erate health at this time hoping that these few lines may find you and yours enjoying good health. After fifty-Six days on the ocean we all landed Safe on new years day and hav all had the fever and I hav lost Felicia but I thank god that our loss Is hur gain. As Job Sais the lord gave and he taketh. I thank god that he has mad it possible that we may meet to part no more. I thank god that we are all on the mend. I cannot tell you much about Liberia. . . . Their is Some that hav come to this place that have got rich and a number that are Sufering. Those that are well off do hav the nativs as

Slavs and poor people that come from america hav no chance to make aliving for the nativs do all the work.[1]

It took little more than a decade before the more prosperous freed slaves bought their own slaves from the indigenous people in West Africa. Freed slaves who didn't have much money hired indigenous people at low wages, making it difficult for new arrivals to earn a decent wage. The new arrivals learned that the ethics of business wasn't much improved from what they left behind in America.

What more could the American Colonization Society expect from the freed slaves than that they would copy the ethics of those in America, who taught them that forced labor was appropriate? It seemed that the freed slaves were willing to make Liberia a Christian nation, and at the same time keep the indigenous people subservient, even to the point of enslaving some of them. The freed slaves apparently did not see the incongruity. From government to schools, from businesses to farming, from religion to relationships, they began to make a new society in Liberia.

Six years later, in another letter to Cocke, Skipworth wrote, "It is something strange to think that these people of Africa are called our ancestors. In my present thinking if we have any ancestors they could not have been like these hostile tribes . . . for you may try and distill [sic] that principle and belief in them and do all you can for them and they still will be your enemy."[2]

Relationships with the indigenous people only deteriorated as the need for additional land grew with more arrivals from America. Just as the white man pushed into new territory occupied by the Indians in America, the freed slaves pushed into territories occupied by the tribesmen, and conflict ensued.

In a scene not unfamiliar to others of that era, in early 1840, the indigenous communities in the vicinity of Heddington attacked a colonial settlement along the St. Paul's River. As many as 400 multi-ethnic tribesmen launched a daybreak attack on the new settlement. Twenty-two of the tribesmen were quickly killed, as the settlers had more advanced weapons. The Monrovian governor, Thomas Buchanan, believed a second attack was inevitable, so he ordered a preemptive strike against the town of Gotorah. The village was burned, but the leader of the tribesman who had killed two of the settlers was not found. Author Claude Clegg III says this kind of skirmish was not unique but became a pattern in the ongoing war over African lands and trade. He wrote, "These attempts by colonists to cauterize indigenous opposition with gunshot and treaties generally proved to be illusory remedies."[3]

During the next twenty years, the colony of freed slaves continued to grow and gain economic stability. Since the colony's establishment, the American Colonization Society had employed white agents to govern it. That changed in 1842 when Joseph Jenkins Roberts became the first non-white governor of Liberia. In 1847, the legislature of Liberia declared itself an independent state, the first on the African continent, with Roberts elected as its first president. In reports former masters received from their former slaves, it is clear that the plan of colonization succeeded for a time, despite setbacks from disease and skirmishes with the natives.

Becoming the Oppressors

The Americo-Liberians showed a remarkable degree of ingenuity—the ability to set up government, build churches, and establish an economy. However, they lacked a healthy sense of self-awareness. They failed to apply the Golden Rule in their relations with the natives. They understood the rule of the slave master. They understood that the man who carries the biggest stick makes the rules. They soon forgot the contempt such an attitude breeds in those who are subjected to the "boss man."

The Liberian people were not aware how self-destructive their contempt for their fellow man would prove. They never saw justice, the rights of the oppressed, issues of power, the pain of having no voice, or economic depravity from the point of view of the indigenous people. Nor did they want to. That was the root of the problem—Americo-Liberians didn't want to know anything about the indigenous people's journey, their feelings, their loss, their pain, or their suffering. The Americo-Liberians didn't want to acknowledge that the indigenous people were people of worth, that their customs had value, that their skills were useful, or that their opinions mattered.

Once the freed slaves left American shores, they left the black/white, slave/free dichotomies and exchanged them for settler/native, Christian/heathen, civilized/uncivilized dichotomies. The freed slaves were given permission to demonize the indigenous people from the beginning. They felt justified in treating them with contempt. Americo-Liberians landed on African shores with a theological mantra called Manifest Destiny: "This is your land. Claim it!"

Struggling for Control

Leading up to the early 1900s, thirteen major conflicts and several minor skirmishes took place between the indigenous people and Americo-Liberians. President Arthur Barclay, Liberia's fifteenth president, shrewdly negotiated an agreement with the kings of the interior (hinterland) and the coast. He convinced them to be brought under the rule of the Americo-Liberians for the first time. The goal was to put a stop to the wars and pacify the indigenous population, while giving their rulers as little power as possible.

A system of authority was set up in the hinterland in which the president of Liberia was the paramount chief, a district commissioner was the big chief, and native kings were quasi-big chiefs. The native kings carried on life as usual. The major difference was that they collected government taxes. They were allowed to keep for themselves any excess taxes. As such, the kings could earn sizable profits. In essence, they became employees of the Liberian government. This centralization of power was most beneficial for the government. It became increasingly authoritarian toward the natives, which led to a general backlash from the indigenous village-states throughout the country and, eventually, to more violence.

The most embarrassing scandal for Liberia internationally, and one that underscored the continued failed efforts of the ruling elite at establishing better relationships with the indigenous population, occurred after the 1927 presidential elections. Defeated presidential candidate Thomas Faulkner accused President-elect Charles D. B. King of allowing slavery to exist in the Republic of Liberia. He also accused certain highly placed government officials of using the Liberian Army to ship laborers to the Spanish island of Fernando Po.

A Committee of the League of Nations was established to examine the allegations. Although the report did not find enough evidence to support the outright claims that the administration was trafficking slaves, sufficient evidence existed that they had abused the compulsory labor system. It was found that they were forcibly recruiting native labor to work on the island of Fernando Po. Both the president and the vice-president resigned in order to avoid being impeached. This incident further hampered relations between the ruling class and the indigenous people.

President Edwin James Barclay succeeded King during a turbulent time. On the one hand, Barclay can be given credit for improving settler-native relations because he gave natives a greater voice in politics, resulting in improved relationships by the early 1940s. On the other hand, Barclay might have created false hope in the indigenous people. They wanted the reforms to continue. Although reforms reached unprecedented levels, Barclay had no intention of compromising the status or dominance of the ruling class.

Presidency under William Tubman

President Barclay's tenure as Liberia's president ended with his retirement in 1944. His successor, William Tubman, was elected in 1944 and served until his death in 1971. The era of President Tubman's presidency is one of the richest in Liberian history. Conflicts between natives and settlers diminished but did not completely disappear. In the post-1931 era, the strict divides of ethnicity between Americo-Liberians, the Congo-man (a term used for the African natives whose slave ships were intercepted in the Atlantic and returned to Liberia, where they formed a community), and the indigenous people became somewhat blurred by intermarriage. This was especially true around Monrovia, though less true in the interior. "Although ethnicity remained a core avenue to power, prestige, and rewards toward the end of the Tubman era, class status and political affiliation ultimately defined the degree to which one could access state power."[4]

Tubman's Open Door Policy gave foreign investors full freedom of entry to the hinterlands, which brought profits and trade opportunities into the interior, benefiting the natives. His Unification Policy granted universal suffrage to hut owners who paid taxes. The number of representatives to the House of Representatives was increased, and the settler-indigenous divide narrowed. Tubman made frequent trips into the interior and became involved in the affairs of the people, even to the point of helping tribes settle disputes.

Even so, the government remained a one-party state, an oligarchic democracy. The government was still ethnically exclusive as far as the power base was concerned. Only a small number of elected positions were reserved for native Liberians. This one-party system continued to deny a place at the political table for indigenous people, fueling resentment and anger that eventually led to Liberia's downfall as a nation. In a true democracy, all people have a voice through a ballot that is open, free, and protected by the government. Liberia's government kept teasing the Liberian natives. Every time the indigenous people tried to take advantage of the democratic process, they were turned away. They were pitched morsels of representation in the government system where there was no power and no ability to bring change to their situation. All the power, all the ability to wield change, remained with the True Whig Party, made up of mostly Americo-Liberians.

An attempt to form a competing party occurred in 1951, when Didwho Twe registered as a presidential candidate for the Reformation Party. Tubman blocked attempts of the party to register, and Twe was forced to flee to Sierra Leone. Afterward, Tubman had term limits thrown out, giving him the right to serve unlimited terms. His stronghold of power gave birth to new lines of contempt within the country. An assassination attempt on Tubman's life in 1955 indicated that the country was becoming unstable, leading Tubman to take extreme measures against any opposition.

Even though people groups began to mix through intermarriage, more division grew along the lines of class. This still often followed lines of ethnicity, but not exclusively. The Tubman government oversaw many changes, but the government had not brought the people together. If anything, by the end of Tubman's presidency, the people were more divided than ever. It was into this atmosphere that President William Tolbert was elected in 1972.

Notes

1. Bill I. Wiley, *Slaves No More—Letters from Liberia* (Lexington: University Press of Kentucky, 1980) 36.

2. William Fitzhugh Brundage, *Where These Memories Grow: History, Memory, and Southern Identity* (Chapel Hill: University of North Carolina Press, 2000) 72.

3. Wiley, *Slaves No More*, 63.

4. Jeremy I. Levitt, *The Evolution of Deadly Conflict in Liberia* (Durham: Carolina Academic Press, 2005) 185.

Chapter 7

Spreading New Seeds of Hope

Seeing Liberia

Olu and I traveled to many points of interest while in Monrovia. Everywhere we traveled, we saw reminders of the pain, suffering, and tragedies of the civil war.

Wherever we traveled in Monrovia, the Economic Community of West African States Cease-fire Monitoring Group (ECOMOG) was visible. They had taken over the Liberian Baptist Theological Seminary campus. Classes on the main campus were suspended and relocated. The main campus was a staging point for these peacekeeping troops appointed by the United Nations. Foxholes formed a border around the buildings of the school. Some damage to the school from the war was still visible. While most of the seminary's office equipment had been destroyed, the buildings were left intact. Also, the library was spared.

When Southern Baptist missionary John Mark Carpenter returned in 1991, the commanding officer of the Ghanaian peacekeeping forces proudly took him to the library to show him the undisturbed books. Reverend Carpenter recalled a phone call his wife, Betty, had received prior to returning in 1991, after having been forced to leave Liberia due to the war. The phone call was from Bert Stician, a missionary who had worked with Betty in Liberia in adult literacy. Bert said to Betty, "Tell John Mark not to worry about that library. I've asked God to build a hedge around it."

The peacekeeping troops, mostly from Nigeria, were friendly. On one occasion, we gave a soldier a ride from the seminary into the city. His machine gun took up quite a bit of room in the back seat I shared with him and a seminary student. A couple of hand grenades on his belt caught my eye. As he talked about his wife and children, it occurred to me that soldiers are mostly the same everywhere. They have the job of protecting their country or someone else's, but mostly their hearts and minds are back home with their families.

Not far from the Liberian Baptist Theological Seminary in the community of Paynesville is Eternal Love Winning Africa (ELWA), an interdenominational Christian campus organization that comprises a radio station, a small hospital, a school, and other local services. This organization partners with churches to promote the gospel.

At the ELWA radio station, I met one of the few missionaries who had returned to his work since the war's outbreak. Most of the missionaries were forced to leave in July 1990 after the National Patriotic Front of Liberia (NPFL) clashed with government troops on the ELWA campus, and most had not returned.[1]

After Olu and I spoke with the young missionary at the radio station, he walked us down to the beach, only a few hundred yards away. He said that during the worst part of the fighting in Monrovia, people in the city fled up the coast toward their radio station in Paynesville. Food was scarce, and the people were desperate for something to eat.

The missionary showed us the beach and told us it had been covered in beautiful coconut palm trees, but as thousands of refugees made their way to Paynesville from Monrovia, the people began to use their machetes to cut down the trees so they could eat the young top portion they called palm cabbage. "In Monrovia itself," he told us, "not too far from the U.S. Embassy in the plush neighborhood of Mamba Point, there was a natural park called Coconut Plantation. It was a breathtaking natural setting, right on the beach, with thousands of palm trees on golden sand. Kids played soccer between the trees, and it was a natural haven to cats and dogs. At the height of the war . . . the inhabitants of Monrovia not only cut down every palm tree to eat the cabbage, but they also killed and ate every single dog and cat that could be found."

The war caused people to resort to such drastic measures just to survive. The education system, which was already typical of a third-world country, took a downward turn. Education was disrupted for months and, in some cases, years. Children had no choice but to drop out of school as the fighting moved from village to village. Eighty percent of the schools prior to 1989 were destroyed during the war.

In Monrovia, soldiers and refugees used schools as compounds and temporary shelters. When the soldiers and displaced people finally left, not much remained of the buildings. Those that reopened years later were in terrible shape. Roofs, windows, equipment, and other materials were missing. There were no functioning lights or toilets. Libraries, laboratories, and playgrounds were gone.

Consequently, Liberia lost the opportunity to educate her children for an entire generation. What did those children do with their lives during the time most of them would have attended school? They learned to stay alive. Thousands of boys were captured and forced to become soldiers. They either fought or they were killed. Thousands of girls and their mothers were raped, and many gave birth. They were forced to raise children they did not need or ask for. In many cases, they didn't even know the name of the child's father.

Most children lost their childhood during the war. Displaced from their homes, along with their families, they spent months in the bush, living off the land, living on the move, living in refugee camps, hoping the fighting would stop, hoping to be able to return home, and hoping to survive another day. There was little time for play. "Normal" became a word of the past.

Liberians spent time oscillating between grief and hope. They experienced great moments of grief. Yet it was overwhelmingly obvious during my time there in 1995 that many still held on to hope.

As we stood there on the beach, the young missionary pointed to a row of coconut palms only about one foot tall. "One of the missionaries recently came here and planted these trees," he said. "He planted the trees as a sign of hope. When people come here in the years ahead, he wants them to see the trees growing and have hope for Liberia's

One of many coconut palms planted as a sign of hope by a missionary in 1995 near the ELWA radio station. These trees now line the beach and are tall and beautiful.

future." The trees planted by the missionary are a sign of hope for people who come to that beach. They grow slowly, but so do the prospects for peace.

A Spirit of Power

Herod, you may recall, had John the Baptist arrested but refused to kill him. He liked having him around. He was intrigued by him. This lasted until the day when Herod, who was drunk at a party, became infatuated with a young girl as she danced before him. She pleased him so much that he made a foolish promise to give her anything she wanted, up to half his kingdom. Excited, no doubt, she ran to her mother with the news. The girl was the daughter of Herodias. She brought back her mother's vengeful request: "John the Baptist's head on a platter."

I find it difficult to read that passage now without thinking about the widowed wife of a Liberian Baptist pastor from Clay First Baptist Church.

Clay, Liberia, is about an hour's drive from the capital city of Monrovia. It is located in Bomi County, just across the Po River. This is the home county of Liberia's current president, Ellen Johnson-Sirleaf. During the civil war, the river was a dividing line between the NPFL and government troops. Three military checkpoints still exist, visible reminders of the tensions that once filled the area between Ricks Institute and the town of Clay.

Clay is a simple town with a marketplace that opens every Friday. It has a government-run school. Catholics and Presbyterians also have churches in the community. Before the war, this community was quiet and peaceful. Clay is a crossroads of sorts. Go northwest and you eventually cross the border to Sierra Leone. Go north and you cross the border into Guinea. The strategic locale made this quiet town vulnerable to brutal rebel forces, helping them cut off routes from people desperate to escape the wrath of a merciless enemy.

When Olu and I arrived at the Baptist church in Clay, I immediately noticed that the main church had sustained damage during the war. A tarp covered partial repairs made to the roof. Rebel forces commonly tore roofs from structures to use the wood. Sometimes they sold it, and other times they burned it. Consequently, thousands of structures in Liberia have walls but no roofs.

Next to the damaged church stood another church made entirely from foliage. This church had a dirt floor with pews constructed from the small trees from the bush. As the pastor showed us the church property, he pointed to the roofless house of the previous pastor at the top of the hill. I imagined it was once a fine home. We were told that the pastor died many years before of natural causes. Later, midway through the worship service, one of the ministers leaned over and told me the story of the pastor's wife. Following her husband's death, she stayed and carried on his responsibilities at the church. When the rebels came, she refused to leave the church property, knowing it would fall into their hands. She vowed to stay and protect it from looters. She was warned about staying, and she paid for her decision with her life: the rebels beheaded her.

For many years, the church services of First Baptist, Clay, were suspended as rebels profaned those grounds with murder and theft. Like a fire that goes out in the night and leaves glowing embers that remain in the morning, the embers of faith left by the pastor, his wife, and the members of First Baptist, Clay, did not go out.

When the people formerly chased from their town returned to their homes, they came back wounded, weary, hungry, broken, and troubled. Yet the embers of their faith still glowed. When they began to remember the faith of their former pastor's wife and the sacrifice she had made, they were encouraged to "fan into flame the gift of God, which is in you. . . . For God did not give us a spirit of timidity, but a spirit of power, of love, and of self-discipline" (2 Tim 1:6-7, NIV).

I saw that power in the people of First Baptist, Clay. Pastor Anderson was one of two men God called from that village to assume ministerial roles at the church. God called a man to play the electric keyboard, powered each Sunday by a generator. God raised up a man to play the drums and another to play the traditional African drum. God raised up a man to play the salsa, a traditional African gourd that sits inside a beaded, webbed container of string and produces a shaker sound when moved around. God raised up a choir to sing and a faithful deaconess who helped me serve the church Holy Communion on the Sunday I preached.

I left knowing God was raising up workers to put the roof back on the church. God is raising up a new generation to hear the gospel, a new generation who can hope that they will no longer experience the horrors of war but only learn of them through the stories of those older than themselves.

From these worshipers at First Baptist, Clay, I was reminded that evil men can kill the body, but they cannot kill the soul (Matt 10:28). Evil men can tear down our places of worship, but they cannot keep us from worshiping God.

Sometimes it takes a while for seeds of hope to germinate and grow, but we must never forget that someone must plant them. God can sling seeds to the wind, but most of the time God looks for someone to sow seeds of hope.

He looks for someone to say, "Here I am, Lord. Send me." If there's one thing Liberia needs, it's people who will sow seeds of hope.

The seeds of compassion and a heart for the people of Liberia were sown within us on our trip in 1995, and especially within Olu as he returned to his home. In his mind, he often saw the faces of the sick, the uneducated, the malnourished, and the dying over the next several years as he continued his studies in the States. God needed shepherds in Liberia willing to take those emerging from the valley of the shadow of death to the green pastures for which they hoped. Over the next decade, God prepared Olu for significant work among his people. The seeds of hope were planted on our trip, and they continued to grow in the years ahead.

Note

1. My visit to the ELWA campus occurred less than four months before the missionaries and Liberian staff were again forced to leave the campus. As rebel forces stormed into Paynesville in April 1996, the building that housed the ELWA radio station was destroyed.

Chapter 8

Reaping a Terrible Harvest

Liberia's Descent into Civil War

Tolbert's Thwarted Attempts at Peace

On September 7, 2007, Star Radio, Liberia, FM 104, reported the death of fifty-nine-year-old Gabriel Baccus Matthews, chairman emeritus of the United People's Party. The station credited Matthews for leading a progressive campaign for a multi-party system in Liberia, resulting in a modern-day party system comprised of more than twenty registered political parties. According to Star Radio, Matthews's life was controversial. Some say he failed as a politician, while others argue that he changed the political landscape of Liberia forever. Actually, both of these statements may be true.

Years before his death, on April 14, 1979, Matthews led about 2,000 people to the executive mansion to peacefully protest the Liberian government's decision to increase the subsidized price of 100 pounds of rice from $22 to $26. The Minister of Agriculture, Florence Chenoweth, had suggested the increase. Her rationale was to force rice farmers to stay on their land and produce more of their own food instead of leaving their farms to venture into the cities or to rubber plantations to find work. Was there another motive? Political opponents thought so. They noted that the families of Chenoweth and President William Tolbert were large-scale rice farmers and stood to profit handsomely from the price increase. Lying deeper beneath the surface of this issue were hostilities that had been growing for decades. The rich were getting richer, while the poor were getting poorer. The Americo-Liberians made money at the expense of the natives who had no voice.

The peaceful protestors who gathered with Matthews were joined by more than 10,000 "back street boys" who quickly transformed the orderly

procession into an orgy of destruction. What followed was later called the
"Rice Riots." Retail stores and rice warehouses were looted, and private property was damaged in excess of $40 million. President Tolbert ordered troops
to quell the rioting. Troops were given orders to storm the headquarters of
the Progressive Alliance of Liberia (PAL). The result was dozens of dead
demonstrators, and more than 500 injured people. The riots drew the attention of neighboring Guinea, whose president dispatched several hundred
troops to assist in restoring order in Monrovia.

Up until the Rice Riots, no opposing party had been allowed to form
since Liberia was established in 1847. The indigenous people of Liberia were
given only token positions in the political process, nothing that carried political weight. As the years went by, more and more of the decision making by
the government began to affect the indigenous people and the "Congo-man"
(African natives whose slave ships were intercepted in the Atlantic and
returned to Liberia, where they formed a community).

President Tolbert held the Progressive Alliance of Liberia leaders and
other political dissidents responsible for the riots. Tolbert, who had sought to
reach out to his political adversaries in some ways, was held responsible by
the old guard for being soft toward his opponents. He was blamed for not
acting sooner to crack down on opposing voices. By most accounts,
President Tolbert was a good man. He was a Christian and an ordained
Baptist minister. In fact, at one time, Tolbert was president of the Baptist
World Alliance, a worldwide gathering of Baptists who seek to unite
Baptists, lead in world evangelism, respond to people in need, defend human
rights, and promote theological reflection.

Tolbert may have become president at a time when it was impossible for
anyone to keep Liberia from splintering. Pressure had built in Liberia for
decades. Even though Tolbert attempted to reach out to his adversaries
through dialogue, it was seen as a token gesture. He continued the policies of
presidents before him and offered no seats of leadership within the government to indigenous people.

Gabriel Baccus Matthews was the first person to challenge openly a deci-
sion by the government. History might have played out differently had the
demonstration remained peaceful. Perhaps Matthews could have become a
Martin Luther King, Jr., figure for Liberia. Just as the peaceful movement of
King set off violence in the United States in places like Montgomery and
Selma, Alabama, Matthews's peaceful intentions rested on top of a powder

keg in Liberia. The explosion of the Rice Riots shook the foundations of the Tolbert presidency.

To restore order, Tolbert temporarily closed the University of Liberia and suspended due process. Chenoweth publicly admitted that she had erred in proposing the price raise, and she was replaced as Minister of Agriculture. Not only was the price of rice not increased; it was reduced from $22 per 100 pounds to $20. After tensions eased, Tolbert granted amnesty to those who were still held in connection with the April rioting and reopened the university. Baccus Matthews, however, was not released.

Tolbert's government had shown a leak in its ability to hold back the mounting pressure of decades of frustration within the indigenous community. Like hyenas stirred by the smell of blood, the enemies of the Tolbert administration saw a weakness that could be exploited and awaited the opportunity.

With the government holding Baccus Matthews, tension ran high. President Tolbert and his government officials were concerned about a potential coup. Their fears came true. On Friday night, April 11, 1980, President Tolbert attended the opening of the Liberian Baptist Missionary and Educational Convention Pavilion at the Centennial Pavilion in downtown Monrovia. It was his custom to travel back to his private residence in Bentol, his hometown just outside Monrovia. However, his security had been tipped off about a possible ambush on the road, so the president decided to retire to the executive mansion instead.

Sometime after midnight, twenty-eight-year-old Master Sergeant Samuel Kanyon Doe led a group of youthful comrades into the mansion. They overpowered the guards and found their way to the room where President Tolbert slept. He was dragged out of bed and dismembered. Later, he was unceremoniously buried in a common grave with two dozen of his security guards. What is not completely clear is how Doe and his men were able to gain such easy access to the president. It remains unclear whether they were provided with outside help.

Samuel Doe's Presidency and Charles Taylor's Ascendancy

Samuel Doe claimed the presidency and, in so doing, became the first indigenous president of Liberia, marking the end of 133 years of Americo-Liberian rule. Doe was an almost illiterate man from the Krahn tribe, which lived deep within the forest of Liberia. He was ill prepared to run a country.

He quickly disposed of many of his enemies, ordering assassinations of thirteen members of William Tolbert's administration. These Liberian leaders paid the ultimate price for Liberia's long history of suppressing and refusing a place at the table of government for the indigenous people. At first, the indigenous people of the country welcomed Doe's coup. "But his government's excessive violations of human rights, over-concentration of power, and rampant and uncontrolled corruption soon turned public opinion against him. His financial mismanagement left Liberia's treasury empty and he shackled the country with nearly two billion dollars in debt."[1]

While the Krahn people account for only about 4 percent of the Liberian population, they made up a disproportionate number of Doe's administration. If keeping power among the Americo-Liberians caused problems among the indigenous people, Doe should have realized that handing out so many positions to the Krahn people would only turn others against him, both indigenous and Americo-Liberian.

The ethicizing and favoritism shown to his own tribe may have become Doe's greatest mistake: "Krahn people were given most of the authority in the military and the most significant posts in the government. The armed forces became almost completely Krahn and behaved more like a faction than a national army. Doe divided ethnic groups as never before."[2] This led to other groups forming with intentions of overthrowing the government and taking it by force. Charles Taylor led one of these groups.

Charles Taylor was an American-educated Liberian from the Gola tribe. During Doe's administration, Taylor was in charge of government purchasing. He was removed after being accused of embezzling nearly one million dollars. He fled to the United States, where he was arrested and imprisoned. Taylor later escaped under suspicious circumstances, made his way back to Africa, put together a guerrilla force, and came into Liberia through the Ivory Coast.

The civil war, the first in the country's nearly 170-year history, began on Christmas Eve of 1989. Charles Taylor and his National Patriotic Front of Liberia (NPFL) launched an invasion through northern Liberia from bases in the Ivory Coast. Taylor's objective was to overthrow the ten-year-old corrupt and dictatorial rule of Doe.

Prince Johnson, originally a member of Charles Taylor's group, broke off and formed his own guerrilla army. He named his group the Independent National Patriotic Front of Liberia (INPFL). On Christmas Eve of 1989, Prince Johnson killed President Samuel Doe in Monrovia and briefly laid claim to the presidency. Unfortunately, this didn't put an end to the war. Neither did it put a stop to lost hopes or dreams. In fact, it only intensified the struggle for control of the country. Before Doe's presidency, the indigenous population suffered. During Doe's presidency, all the Americo-Liberian population suffered. Following Doe's death, nothing could prepare the country for what came next.

The war shifted from one of revolution to one of genocide. Civilians were killed in far greater numbers than combatants. They were subjected to arbitrary arrest, detention, harassment, torture, rape, mutilation, and executions. Children were no exception. The use of child soldiers under the age of fifteen became an unfortunate characteristic of this conflict introduced by Charles Taylor. Children were drugged before going to the battlefield. Taylor's flagrant disregard for human rights and the despotic nature of his rule continued to carry the country deeper into despair. The war killed close to 300,000 Liberians, displaced about 1,000,000 persons, and sent more than 800,000 into refugee camps around the sub-region. About one out of every ten Liberians died during the war.

When one tries to understand the genesis of the Liberian civil war, a case can be made that the seeds for the war began as early as the attitudes and practices of the Americo-Liberians who demonstrated that they were superior in every way to the indigenous population. Nearly 150 years of domination created a ticking time bomb that was handed down from generation to generation until it finally exploded. Had you looked carefully at that time bomb, you might have found these words: "Parts Made in America: Assembled in Liberia."

The freed slaves took on the attitude of superiority that their masters had imposed on them and transferred the practices of it to the native people of the land they were settling. This understanding of how social systems work had been modeled for them. They were even taught that it could be justified by their Christian faith.

Notes

1. Veronica Nmoma, "The Civil War and the Refugee Crisis in Liberia," *The Journal of Conflict Studies* 17/1 (Spring 1997), http://www.lib.unb.ca/Texts/JCS/bin/get.cgi?directory= SPR97/articles/&filename=nmoma.html.
   2. Ibid.

Chapter 9

Being Home; Going Home

Dangerous Memories

In the 1990s, "suppressed memory" dominated the headlines. The Supreme Court had to rule whether cases could be tried when a witness suddenly remembered a crime he or she had suppressed for years, even decades. Even Lucy from the "Peanuts" comic strip weighed in on the issue: "The fact that you can't remember being abducted by aliens and satanically abused," she told Charlie Brown, "is proof that it really happened."[1]

Despite the controversy over using such evidence in courts, the American Psychiatric Association recognizes memory suppression as a legitimate malady: "It makes perfect logical sense that children who've been traumatized and abused would have to sort of hide those memories away rather than confront them."[2] It also makes logical sense that people bury traumatic events until memories are triggered by other events that happen later in life.

Trained counselors are taught to look for these events in a person's past that may cause problems without rising to the recognizable surface. Sometimes counselors don't have to look far, as these memories come rushing back during sessions. They may also arise at unexpected times, triggered by a smell, the sight of an old photograph, the visit of someone who reminds them of a person from the past, or the sight of a place where trauma occurred.

Olu Menjay's return to Monrovia in 1995 was a mixture of joy and what he described as "dangerous memories." He saw old friends and visited places that brought back memories of the days of his youth and the months of fighting that nearly claimed his life. Much had changed since his last visit. Many people he knew had died. Many who had left Monrovia had not returned. Many forced from their homes had resettled in other places. Few buildings in Monrovia stood unblemished from the war.

One day as we drove along the road in Monrovia, Olu suddenly said, "Right there is where I saw my first rotting body. Dogs were feeding on the rotten flesh." It was one of those suppressed memories that suddenly rose to the surface, brought about by the sight of the location of a gruesome event.

Olu had lived in exile for six years except for the brief time he left the Ivory Coast to meet Reverend John Mark Carpenter in Liberia to get money for a ticket to the United States. During his exile, he often thought of Liberia but learned to block out as many painful memories as possible. He experienced great joy in his trip back to Liberia in 1995, but nothing held back the flood of memories he had suppressed all those years. Pain tempered his delight in seeing his family.

In the early stages of Olu's Ivory Coast exile, the pain was fresh. In fact, during his first two years in that country, every day involved a struggle for survival. Once he made it to the United States, Olu's physical needs were met and he allowed his mind to rest. The wounds were still open, but as with most who are exiled, the longer he lived away from the violence, the pain, the hunger, and the stench of death, the easier it became to suppress the haunting memories and build a new life.

Although those in exile may become increasingly homesick, they learn to adapt to their new surroundings. Most become survivors. Like the Jews carried into Babylon, they learn to fit into their new surroundings. They acquire new skills and learn how to live productive lives. While they continue to have thoughts of home, most try to suppress painful memories.

As we traveled through Liberia, Olu and I hoped for God to teach us. We were not disappointed. Olu's trip back to Liberia relit his candle of hope for his country. Olu had traveled back home many times in his mind. However, nothing equaled physically going back to places of his youth, some of them joyful and some painful. During our trip, Olu was reminded of what he loved about his country. He reveled in the worship, which he had longed for and missed while in the States. He rejoiced in the customs unique to his country. He began to revert back to the fast-paced Liberian English when gathered with his friends. There was lots of laughter in the presence of his loved ones. I knew Olu was more at home there than he ever was in America. He had missed the Liberian food, and although there certainly wasn't an abundance of it, it tasted far better than anything he ate in America. The trip to Liberia reminded Olu that he was a Liberian. Once again, he knew where his heart belonged.

Of course, not everything about the trip was joyful. Every day Olu and I passed St. Peter's Lutheran Church, where troops loyal to former president Samuel Doe had massacred at least 600 people, most of them women and children who took refuge in the church. They had traveled to Monrovia on foot to escape the fighting in their home county of Nimba. Even though these displaced people were no threat to Doe and his men, on the evening of July 29, 1990, 200 of his soldiers walked along the beach to St. Peter's Lutheran Church, where they slaughtered those inside. Some reports place President Doe at the scene during the massacre.

The injustice done to his people, the government's squandering of the country's resources, the waste of human resources and human potential all angered Olu. The conditions in the country had deteriorated far beyond what he had imagined. There was no running water and no electricity. The effects of the absence of basic services of life were difficult to imagine until we saw them firsthand. Olu had serious questions about Liberia's future: "Will Liberia be restored? Will there be any sense of peace? Will I be able to return and serve?"

After suppressing his memories while studying and living in America, Olu became increasingly angry the longer he stayed in Monrovia and witnessed the poverty, the constant military checkpoints and searches, the people begging for food, the children working instead of going to school, his family without electricity, and the lack of running or safe drinking water.

To make matters worse, Olu's friends and family looked to him as their hope. In their eyes, he had been to the "promised land." Just as the people had gathered at the airport looking for a relative or someone who was willing to give them something, Olu soon discovered he was the focus of attention in an unexpected way. Every evening as he went back to his parents' home, a group of people waited for him to plead their case as if he had money to hand out to every person who came to see him.

To these people, one American dollar was a lot of money. The average income during the war for a Liberian citizen was about $150 per year. Olu was simply a poor Liberian attending college in America, but he could not make these people understand that he did not have the resources to help them. They still approached him each day.

One day Olu came to the Baptist Missionary Compound (later named the Dorothy Pryor Compound after the National Women's Missionary Union leader) where I stayed, and he shared his frustration of not being able to meet the needs of people who thought he could help them simply because he had been in America. One of the missionaries smiled and said, "Now you know what it feels like to be white." Laughter ensued.

Despite this, the longer Olu stayed, the more his Liberian nature returned. He remembered that he had escaped Liberia by God's grace and he began to feel stronger than ever that it would be an honor to serve his people if God made it possible for him to return. Stumps of war, hunger, rape, murder, torture, and homelessness dominated the landscape. We knew we worshiped a "Green Shoot God," a God who specializes in sending green shoots from stumps. Though it wasn't said aloud, I knew deep down that Olu wanted to return to Liberia for good, but at that time, the tree was still being cut down.

Olu looked for hope in Liberia, but as he prepared to leave, most of what he saw pointed him in a different direction. Liberia wasn't making progress. The big question Olu faced was the same question asked by most people who leave third-world countries for America, Europe, and other addresses of safety and abundance: "Should I hope for something better in America where life is easier and opportunities are greater, or should I hope to return to this troubled place and make sacrifices that will bring green shoots from the stumps of my country?"

In 1995, Olu didn't know the answer to that question. He grieved what Liberia had lost. His country was still in the process of losing her people, her resources, and the ability to live without fear, the threat of death, starvation, and disease. The people lived under President Charles Taylor, a president who would later be charged by the War Crimes Tribunal at The Hague for crimes committed against the people in Sierra Leone and who would later retreat into exile because of his treatment of his own people.

Where was the Liberian church during these times? The church was sitting where Job sat, on the ash heap protesting, lamenting, and crying out to God. Within the church's worship, it struggled to hold on to its faith. Like the psalmist, the church in Liberia rediscovered its faith through rebellious worship.

Liberia is still in this process of allowing God to unlock the fetters of the civil

The eyes of this naked child are intently focused on his mother who lives in the internal displacement (refugee) camp on the Ricks campus.

war and reclaim the goodness of her past. In the 1990s, church buildings in Liberia sat empty and silent for months as people were driven from their homes and communities. Some church buildings were used as temporary shelters for displaced people, and rebels took over others. However, the church is not made up of buildings, but of people. Although the Liberian church was scattered, exiled, and displaced, the people still worshiped God. In fact, they may have worshiped God more honestly than ever. As the church struggled, laments came freely. As the people joined together and remembered those they had lost, as they remembered the days prior to the war, as they read Scriptures and remembered the songs of the faith, surprisingly they found hope.

Leaving Liberia

As our trip neared its end, my memories turned to my wife and small children who anxiously awaited my return. Christmas Day drew near. I boarded the small plane back to Abidjan without Olu. He chose to remain behind for another ten days. An ordination council was assembled, waiting to question him and to judge his qualifications for ordination as a minister of the gospel in the Baptist denomination.

My gratitude for the experience of being in Liberia was exceeded only by my gratitude of sitting on a plane headed for the United States. Of course, I couldn't get to the United States directly from Monrovia. It was a long process of backtracking.

Without Olu by my side, I was anxious as I boarded the plane in Monrovia. I had to stop in the Ivory Coast, a French-speaking country. Making the connecting flight from Abidjan to Paris was my only chance to get home by Christmas Day.

I was leaving a country where people's main concerns were escaping gunfire, finding food and fresh water, and securing a place to sleep each night. I thought about the differences in their lives and mine. My main concern that day was getting on the next flight so I could open presents with my family on Christmas. There was a great difference in our two worlds.

Just being alone in Abidjan gave me a deeper appreciation for the survival skills of displaced people who cross borders. Often they must learn another language and the customs and laws of another nation, with the disadvantages of no bank account, credit card, job, cash, visa, passport, or plane ticket to escape their condition.

I had seen this up close even before Olu and I arrived in Liberia. Less than two weeks earlier, during our one-night layover in Abidjan as we made our journey to Liberia, I was surprised when Olu's brother Hugo showed up at the Baptist compound where we spent the night.

Olu had contacted his brother Hugo days before we left the United States, informing him of our layover. Like Olu, Hugo had escaped the violence in Liberia and was exiled in a refugee camp. Instead of the Ivory Coast, he was in Ghana. He spent days walking and hitchhiking in order to meet us at the Baptist Compound in Abidjan. Not long after we arrived, Olu and Hugo were reunited for the first time in six years.

I sat in our room and watched two brothers embrace and love each other. I watched as Olu opened his luggage. Hugo went through it and took as many clothes as Olu could spare. Olu gave Hugo his watch, and they shared a Coke from the 1950s-era icebox in our room. As Hugo prepared to leave, I gave him money. I had an empty feeling as I watched him slip into the darkness with Olu. I wondered what would happen to him. What did his future hold? Would he survive the harsh environment of the refugee camp? Would Olu ever see him again?

Now, back in Abidjan and on my way to America, I faced trouble just as I'd feared when trying to negotiate my connecting flight home since I could not speak French. I was thankful that a Southern Baptist missionary agreed to come to the airport and be my interpreter. She helped me solve my ticket problem and make my flight home.

As I settled into a comfortable seat on a plane headed toward Paris, I thought of watching my children play with their toys on Christmas morning. What a contrast from the country I'd left, where the children I met had never awakened to a morning full of new playthings. The children I had met would have been happy simply if their memories of Christmas from that point on could be filled with "peace on earth and goodwill toward men."

Olu's Ordination and Return to the United States

While I returned to the United States to enjoy Christmas with my family, Olu stayed in Liberia to spend more time with his family and to appear before an ordination council.

If you walk into the offices of most Baptist ministers, you see on the walls their framed credentials, which usually include a degree from a college and a seminary, a certificate of license to the gospel ministry, and a certificate of ordination. Of these, the framed ordination certificate comes the closest to representing a minister's calling to vocational ministry.

Olu's ordination in Liberia followed the typical format of ordination in Baptist churches in the States, evidence of the influence of the work of Southern Baptist missionaries in Liberia. As in the United States, the ordination council comprised ordained clergy from the immediate area of the church where Olu was to be ordained.

The job of the ordination council is to question the candidate on issues of calling, doctrine, morality, integrity, family issues, or any subject the council feels is important for carrying out the duties of being a minister of the gospel. The council awards the candidate an ordination certificate after judging that the candidate has the gifts, calling, and satisfactory biblical doctrine to be publicly set apart and ordained to the work of the gospel ministry. A date is then set for the official ceremony where the "laying on of hands" occurs. This is a moving experience for the one being ordained as members of the congregation and others of the Christian faith known to the candidate come forward to lay hands on his or her head and pray.

At New Georgia Baptist Church, Olu met with the church's pastor, Rev. Kormah Dorko; Rev. Olayee Collins, pastor of Providence Baptist Church; Rev. Marculey Jarbah, pastor of Bridgeway Baptist; Rev. Abraham Fully, pastor of Shiloh Baptist Church; and Olu's father, Rev. Harrison Menjay, pastor of Second Providence Baptist Church.

The men asked Olu questions like these: What is a distinct mark of being Baptist? Tell us why the priesthood of all believers is important. What is the significance of the autonomy of the local church? Tell us about your own faith journey. How did you get to where you are in your spiritual pilgrimage? Share your calling experience.

Olu gave satisfactory answers to these questions and many others until they asked him to define sin. Olu responded, "Sin is anything that separates us from God." Olu didn't cloud the definition with examples of sin, figuring the pastors could supply their own. However, the council wasn't satisfied. They wanted Olu to name sins. Apparently, they had a list and wanted to see if Olu's list matched theirs.

When Olu refused to play their matching game and simply stood by his definition, the council grew uneasy. They suspected Olu might be hiding a liberal agenda with his evasive answer. This prompted a major discussion among the council. Olu showed great resolve in holding firm to his convictions. He stood in front of his spiritual fathers and peers. While they agreed on most issues of the faith, they found an area that opened the door for good theological dialogue and some disagreement. Olu could have easily folded on his point simply to move along his ordination process, but in holding firm, he demonstrated one of the core freedoms we cherish as Baptists—Bible freedom, a cherished Baptist distinctive that stresses that each person must wrestle with the biblical text, interpret the text, and seek to live out the text in a manner pleasing to God.

From Olu's study of the Bible, he saw sin, any sin, as that which separates us from God. The ordination council wanted to find out whether Olu's specific list of sins matched their specific list of sins without asking him specifically. Olu held firm: "Any sin," he said, "separates us from God." In the end, the council, though not completely comfortable with his answer, could find no fault with it since it didn't contradict Scripture. They gave Olu their blessing and signed his ordination certificate.

The following Sunday, a service of ordination was held for Olu at New Georgia Baptist Church, a church created in the 1980s by the partnership between Georgia Baptists, U.S.A., and the Liberia Baptist Missionary and Education Convention. During the ordination, Olu's father, Rev. Harrison Menjay, presented him with a new Bible and quoted Luke 2:29-30: "Lord, now lettest thou thy servant depart in peace, according to thy word: for mine eyes have seen thy salvation" (KJV). This was Rev. Menjay's way of expressing his pleasure in having the opportunity to live long enough to see one of his children called into the ministry. Should his life be taken, it had been a full life.

In the six years since the war began, Olu had seen his mother and father for only a couple of days. On this trip, receiving his father's blessing was a priceless gift. His relationship with his Heavenly Father was blessed and affirmed by his earthly father, whom he loved and respected. His father was a man greatly respected throughout Liberia, even outside Baptist circles. Like so many in Liberia, the Menjays had lost much during the war. This was a moment to savor.

Within a few days, Rev. Olu Menjay packed his bags and bid his parents and his friends a painful goodbye. He traveled to the small airport in Monrovia, expecting an uneventful flight back to the Ivory Coast. From there, he would make the long backtracking journey to the United States. However, Rev. Olu Menjay was reminded of the fragility of peace in Monrovia and the surrounding areas. When he arrived at the airport, his flight to the Ivory Coast was cancelled as fighting broke out in the city, delaying him for three days. If that had happened a couple of weeks earlier and I had been stranded at the airport for three days without a way out, I think I might have left my zeal for missions in Monrovia.

Rev. Olu Menjay took it in stride. He was inconvenienced, but he never panicked during the ordeal. He said, "As long as you are alive, you always have hope." Although it was fearful to listen to gunfire again, there was some level of hope that a plane would arrive and he would be able to board a flight back to the United States.

A few days later, a plane came in bound for Guinea, not for the Ivory Coast where Rev. Menjay needed to make his connecting flight. Guinea was in the opposite direction, but sometimes you "can't get there (wherever *there* is) from Liberia." Rev. Menjay took the flight to Guinea. From there, he caught another flight to the Ivory Coast, then to Dakar, to Paris, and on to the United States.

Notes

1. Mary Carmichael, "An Irrepressible Idea," *Newsweek* 19 January 2004, http://www.newsweek.com/id/52790.

2. Dahlia Lithwick (with Madeleine Brand), "Slate's Jurisprudence: Repressed Memories and the Courts," NPR Special, 2 February 2005, http://www.npr.org/templates/story/story.php?storyId=4490707.

Chapter 10

"Lettest Thou Thy Servant Depart in Peace"

They Left Their Home in Haste

Two years before our trip to Liberia, ECOMOG formed the security buffer around Monrovia. As fighting increased around Liberia, Monrovia became a haven to a million people, a third of the country's population. To protect the people, ECOMOG, mostly made up of Nigerian troops, sealed off the city.

During our time in Liberia, Rev. Menjay and I were constantly reminded of the fragile peace process. The peacekeeping troops were everywhere in the city with checkpoints every few miles. Once, we were stopped and forced to get out of our car. We were asked to open our trunk, and the soldiers questioned us.

Often, these stops were little more than harassment and a means for the soldiers to make money. Corruption is rampant in third-world countries. Soldiers and policemen often make money by stopping people and demanding payment before allowing them to continue. Farmers bringing produce into the city are often pulled over at checkpoints, where they are forced to pay a fee to continue into the city to sell their goods.

The armored vehicles driven by peacekeeping troops signaled the presence of the international peacekeeping force. I wondered whether they would fight in a real crisis. Would these men sacrifice their lives to protect Monrovia and her people?

In the earliest stages of the Liberian civil war, the battle lines fell more clearly along indigenous and Americo-Liberian skirmishes. Problems between these people groups were the sparks that ignited flames of discontent. The highly charged struggles between these two groups in Liberia led Samuel Doe, twenty-eight years old and mostly illiterate, to assassinate

President William Tolbert, becoming the first indigenous president of the country. However, over the ten years he remained president and during the years Charles Taylor held power, the reasons for the fighting in Liberia became less defined.

By 1996, seven warring factions all fought for a slice of the Liberian pie, for power and loot. Some were not even sure why they fought. Even though more than thirteen peace accords were signed, the fighting resumed in Monrovia in April 1996. ECOMOG abandoned their posts, and the battle for Monrovia was on. Over the next seven weeks, 1500 people died in the city. In the end, Charles Taylor emerged as the dominant power. The people who had moved into the city looking for safety scattered again during the renewed fighting, searching desperately for places of refuge.

It's difficult to comprehend this kind of fear. Perhaps American survivors of natural disasters can relate. In Southern California, people live with the constant threat of wildfires. A lifetime of work and memories can disappear quickly as flames leap from one hillside to another, consuming whatever is in their path. One woman describes the flames of a 1993 fire as they came closer and closer to her home:

> It started with a call from a friend in Riverside. I ran out to the street and saw red flames piercing the sky on the eastern side of the canyons. I raced back into the house thinking about packing and tried to emotionally prepare to release all of my material possessions . . . . I ran from room to room trying to figure out what was important. Should I get my papers, the baby shoes, how about the souvenirs from a lifetime of traveling? And if I'm going to be living in a shelter for months, maybe I should take a toothbrush and a change of clothes. Finally, I packed the computer into the car along with my personal papers but then went back to running in circles. Everything was important. I tried to flood my eyes with the memories of my life. I could see flames leaping from the mountain peaks less than a mile away. I watched friends move their horses. Around 1 a.m., two girlfriends came over and we sat through the night drinking wine and trying to entertain each other, but the nervous laughter could not hide our fears. When they left, I decided to sleep in my clothes. It's a new day and the planes have been flying since dawn dropping fire retardant. Friends keep coming by telling me to leave. Things are getting worse nearby. The fire has jumped to my side of the canyon.[1]

Replace the fear of flames with fear of gunfire and mayhem, and you may capture some of the emotions of those trapped in the limbo of civil war.

As the rebels advanced on Monrovia in April 1996, shortly after Rev. Menjay returned to the States as an ordained minister, his parents, Rev. Harrison and Ella Menjay, were among those who hastily gathered their belongings to leave, not knowing if or when they would return.

Rev. Harrison and Ella Menjay had to leave their home quickly, taking only what they could carry. When would they return? They didn't know. What would they find when they returned? They didn't know. Usually, when people returned, everything of value was gone.

As they left, Rev. Menjay failed to get his medication for an illness he had suffered for several months. Though not confirmed, it is believed that he had tuberculosis, a life-threatening disease that primarily infects the lungs. The tuberculosis bacterium grows slowly, so treatment for the infection is lengthy, usually six to twelve months.

When the Menjays left Monrovia, they went to New Kru Town, an area outside of Monrovia proper, to find refuge with relatives. They were gone for almost three months. Without his medicine, Rev. Menjay had little hope of getting better. His condition worsened. Finally, in July, he and his wife were able to return to Monrovia. By this time, disease had ravaged Rev. Menjay's body.

In October 7, 1996, Rev. Olu Menjay received a fax at Duke Divinity School informing him that his father had died. Rev. Harrison Menjay was fifty-eight years old. Although the numbers of fatalities from the Liberian civil war do not count such people, the war cut Rev. Harrison Menjay's life short, just as it did an untold number like him. Because of a lack of access to doctors and medicine to treat curable diseases, tens of thousands died in addition to the 250,000 who died as a direct result of violence. Many are still dying, making the life expectancy for a Liberian male only 40.7 years in the year 2000. Life expectancy has risen only slightly since then.

Rev. Harrison Menjay may have had some premonition that his life was not long for this world. Perhaps that's why he used prophetic words at his son's ordination service: "Lord, now lettest thou thy servant depart in peace, according to thy word."

Rev. Harrison Menjay lived a faithful life as God's servant. He was an educator both in the school system and in the church, serving people his entire life. He went to Zorzor Rural Training Institute for Teachers. He taught for a while before studying on a scholarship at the Nigerian Baptist Theological Seminary. He served for more than twenty years as principal of a junior high school in Nimba and also as an assistant pastor there. He pastored Second Providence Baptist Church in Monrovia for twelve years. Rev. Menjay was passionate about education, and he wanted all of his children to receive the best education possible. Sadly, it took a civil war for him to see his son receive that kind of education.

The Duke Divinity School was supportive of their newly ordained Liberian native. Dean Dennis Campbell granted Rev. Olu Menjay leave from school to return to Liberia to bury his father. The tradition in Liberia is to wait about three weeks after death before burial. Olu arrived one week before the service. With all of his family present, along with trustees of the Liberian Baptist Theological Seminary and pastors from many churches in the Monrovia area, Rev. Menjay preached his father's funeral at Second Providence Baptist Church.

His message, from Psalm 1, spoke about the need to be trustworthy in the midst of suffering and pain. Olu praised his father as a man of integrity who served God and humanity fearlessly. He said his father delighted in God's word. He was like a "tree planted by streams of water" (Ps 1:3).

In attendance at the funeral was the associate pastor, Emmanuel Wlue, who sat beside me in that same church just ten months earlier. Now much of the responsibility for shepherding the flock would fall on his young shoulders.

Within a week following his father's funeral, Rev. Olu Menjay said farewell to his family and friends and made his way back to the United States to continue his education and ministry. With the conditions the way they were, it didn't seem likely that he would return to Liberia and help his people. It was his prayer that Liberia would one day live up to her name, "land of the free," and be free of war, free of starving people, free of people who died of treatable diseases, free of fear so people wouldn't have to leave their homes, and free of hatred that separated Liberian from Liberian.

Liberia still had dark years ahead before good news began to seep out. Just seven months after the funeral of Rev. Harrison Menjay, word came that the young associate pastor, Emmanuel Wlue, had also died, another death from complications of disease in an unforgiving land. Second Providence had lost both of her leaders.

My mind reflected back to the day I sat at Second Providence Baptist and Emmanuel leaned over to me and said, "Thank you for bringing hope to us." I recalled Rev. Harrison Menjay's words to me following the message: "Thank you for bringing to us the 'thus saith the Lord.'"

Their deaths shook me. When we hear of people suffering and dying in third-world countries, it's easy to feel disconnected, to go about our routine. The deaths of these men affected me because I knew them and because they were doing the Lord's work. Of all people, these men brought hope to their people. They brought the "thus saith the Lord."

Losing them was a reminder that God's servants are prone to sickness and suffering. God's people are not bullet proof. While God may put a hedge around some at times, we all serve God with no guarantee of tomorrow. Our only guarantee is that God will never leave us or forsake us. Reading of the persecution of the early church can remind us of the sacrifices of Christians through the ages. It's easy to forget when we practice our faith with so little resistance.

Associate Pastor Emmanuel Wlue proudly holds a picture of his father, Rev. D. Kennedy Wlue, a former pastor of Second Providence Baptist Church. Emmanuel died the year after our visit.

When Rev. Olu Menjay returned from burying his father, I wondered if he'd ever go back to follow in his father's footsteps. Would the country ever stabilize enough to allow him that possibility? If it did, would Olu Menjay make the sacrifice to go?

Note

1. Donna Mungeon, interview by Noah Adams, "What Do You Take When the House Is Burning Down?" *All Things Considered*, NPR, 28 October 1993.

Chapter 11

Living a Life of Significance

Progress in Liberia and Dr. Menjay's Return

Olu's remaining years at Duke Divinity School were a time of great theological growth. Following seminary, he pursued advanced theological degrees from Boston University and a doctorate from the University of Wales through the International Baptist Theological Seminary in Prague, Czech Republic. He worked with Rev. Dr. John Fuller, sharpening his skills in the pulpit twice a month, assisting with church administration duties, and learning how to diplomatically decline offers from members to fix him up with dates while serving at Lewis Chapel Church.

Throughout his studies, Dr. Menjay related his academic work to a Liberian context.[1] If he was writing a paper about pastoral leadership, he wrote it in the Liberian context. If he wrote about pastoral care, he wrote in the Liberian context. As he did, he imagined returning to Liberia as a professor. His passion was Christian missions. If you asked him to define his calling, he might have said, "I feel called to teach Christian missions."

The Southern Baptist missionary movement in Liberia left a distinct stamp on Liberian Baptists, including Dr. Menjay. Rev. John Mark Carpenter worked as a missionary among the people in Sinoe County, the southeastern part of Liberia. Dr. Menjay's parents were among those Rev. Carpenter discipled and led to a deeper understanding of Christ. He also led them in the exchange of their wedding vows. Later, Rev. Carpenter was the missionary responsible for rescuing Olu from the refugee camp in the Ivory Coast and getting him to the United States to study at Truett-McConnell.

Dr. Menjay is a product of missions. He has seen missions done well. He has seen missions done poorly. He has researched missions from a historical, theological, and pragmatic perspective. As his vocational interest and calling developed, it all pointed him to becoming a teacher in a seminary setting with missions as a focus.

As he approached the conclusion of his work at Duke Divinity School, the political landscape in Liberia had improved. Former Liberian leader Charles Taylor was exiled to Nigeria in 2003. A peace agreement in Liberia was negotiated. A transitional government was put in place until democratic elections could be held to elect a new president.

Taylor went to Nigeria with the government's promise that they would not turn him over to the United Nations court, who wanted him on charges of war crimes against Sierra Leone. As Taylor prepared to board the plane, he said, "I leave you with these parting words: God willing, I will be back." Although Taylor was leaving, it was clear that he did not think his influence or hold on the country was lost forever.

The presidential election was held in October 2005. Out of the twenty-two candidates (representing twenty-two different political parties), George Weah, a former international soccer star, and Ellen Johnson-Sirleaf, a Harvard-educated woman and former World Bank employee who also had served at one point as Liberia's finance minister, qualified for a runoff. The second election was held on November 8. Johnson-Sirleaf received nearly 60 percent of the vote, becoming Africa's first democratically elected female head of state.

Perhaps Johnson-Sirleaf's election was as much a reward for her faithfulness to Liberia as it was a reflection of any of her promises during the campaign. She had been a part of the Tolbert administration but was not serving with him at the time of his assassination. Following his assassination and fearing for her life, she had left Liberia and had gone into exile for a number of years. Bravely, she came back into the country to run against Samuel Doe in the mid-1980s, but she was promptly jailed. As it turned out, Doe had rigged the elections anyway, and Johnson-Sirleaf had no chance to win. While in jail, she says, she lived under the threat of rape and execution. Because of her fearlessness and her iron will in the face of danger, the people of her country refer to her as the "iron lady."

Johnson-Sirleaf's election brought hope to Liberians, including many who had been exiled, like Dr. Olu Menjay. Her election gave Liberians hope for a stable political future. Dr. Menjay seriously began to consider a return home. He wrote a letter to the president of the Liberian Baptist Theological Seminary, Dr. Lincoln Brownell, in hopes of finding a teaching position available at the seminary, but the letter was never acknowledged. He followed that letter with one to Rev. Emile Sam-Peale, executive secretary of the Liberian Baptist Missionary and Education Convention, about his desire to return to Liberia. They discussed the challenges his desire presented as well as the possibilities.

Rev. Sam-Peale said to Dr. Menjay, "Why don't you consider coming to Ricks and being the principal?"

Dr. Menjay thought he was joking and replied that he couldn't go to Ricks.

Wisely, Sam-Peale offered, "You might just want to come and see what can happen." He then wrote Dr. Menjay a letter asking him to come and accept the position as principal of Ricks Institute.

Founded in 1887, the school is named for Moses U. Ricks, who migrated in 1852 from Petersburg, Virginia, at the age of twenty-five. He brought along his family under the auspices of the American Colonization Society. Over the next thirty-five years, he became a successful coffee farmer. At the age of sixty, Ricks, a Baptist, donated $500 to the Liberian Baptist Missionary and Education Convention to purchase land for a school. He believed educational and missional success in Liberia rested on the people of Liberia.

From the beginning, the philosophy and the mission of the school reflected the work of African missionaries such as Lott Cary, Alexander Crummell, and Edward Blyden. These men believed free educational opportunities should be carried to the indigenous people of the country, including females. Their philosophy heavily influenced the beginning of Ricks Institute, which started as a boarding school. The school charged for room and board but not for instruction. Students were admitted regardless of their religious affiliation; good moral character and sound physical health were requirements for enrollment.

Dr. Menjay accepted the invitation to go to Liberia for a look. He traveled with three African-American preachers, Dr. Matthew A. Rouse, Jr.; Rev. T. W. Campbell; and Rev. Jesse L. Timmons, all from North Carolina, who went to Liberia to conduct revival meetings. One of the meetings was held at New Georgia Baptist Church.

When they arrived at the gate of Ricks Institute, the first thing Dr. Menjay noticed was that the grass was taller than he was. The challenges were visible to everyone. One of the preachers said, "Menjay, do you really want to do this? You can always go back to North Carolina and serve with John Fuller [pastor of Lewis Chapel Missionary Baptist Church]."

The ministers noted the damage to the campus from the war. The buildings had no windows. Roofs leaked and ceilings were destroyed. It was discouraging. Dr. Menjay's initial reaction was to leave and return to the States. More discouraging than the physical damage was his conversation with those who knew the financial condition of the school. The school had less than $200 in the bank. The teachers were owed almost six months' salary. The average teacher's salary was $17 per month, and a 100-pound bag of rice cost $24. A healthy Liberian family of five can consume *two* 100-pound bags of rice a month.

Realistically, Dr. Menjay knew he shouldn't take the position. Then he said to himself, "All I can do is try; just try one building at a time. If I am unsuccessful, then at least I tried. If I think I am too good for this position, who is it for? If I don't do it, who will do it?"

Rebuilding Ricks

Dr. Menjay met with the Educational Commission in charge of Ricks and other schools owned by the Liberian Missionary and Education Convention. The commission had big dreams for Ricks. They wanted Ricks to reopen the junior college that had once been a part of the school. The school closed when war came to the campus, and following the war, the university building began filling up with displaced people. Those on the commission shared their dreams with Dr. Menjay, perhaps trying to impress him.

Finally, they turned to him and asked about his dreams and visions for the institution. Dr. Menjay said, "My vision is for us to cut the grass." This was hardly the answer they expected. Dr. Menjay decided not to play the game of being profound. Instead he decided to be realistic. He knew that something as simple as cutting the grass would create a sense of human dignity and pride among those who lived on campus and those who went to school there. He didn't intend to live in a fantasyland. Instead, he decided to think small with the anticipation of accomplishing something significant. In doing so, he also showed the commission something of his nature.

Dr. Olu Menjay's middle name is Quaity. In his native Sarpo language, it means "meekness." Taking a job as principal of Ricks Institute was a lesson in humility. As he sat with the Educational Commission of the school, he chose not to begin their relationship by pretending the job didn't entail starting with the fundamentals of service. The group did not expect a reverend to talk about cutting grass, but neither did Jesus' disciples expect him to wear a towel and wash their feet.

As word spread that Dr. Menjay had taken the job at Ricks, there was a mixed response. A cousin came to visit him at the school and tried to persuade him to leave. "You can get a government position. It makes no sense to do what you are doing. You need to fold it up." Dr. Menjay acknowledged, "Everything [my cousin] said about the school was right." Everything, that is, except his assessment of the school's future.

Dr. Menjay believed he could make a difference. In choosing to accept the job, he thought about the significance of lives like Mother Teresa. She never served in what the world may call significant places, like Washington, D.C., or New York City. She stayed in Calcutta and made a difference. Likewise, when Martin Luther King, Jr., began his ministry, he left Boston University. He had an opportunity to serve in Atlanta as co-pastor with his father. Instead, he went to Montgomery to serve an impoverished, "insignificant" church. "That told me, 'Listen, man, you can stay right here in Liberia and make a difference at Ricks,'" says Menjay.

Believing in his calling, the people of Lewis Chapel Missionary Baptist Church in Fayetteville, North Carolina, gave Menjay the initial financial support he needed. They were his backbone. Dr. John Fuller was his encourager. "I had their prayer and financial support," Dr. Menjay says. From there, he began to connect with other partners who might come and assist in his dream to rebuild Ricks. In fact, if Ricks is rebuilt on anything, it is rebuilt on relationships.

The first relationships Dr. Menjay had to rebuild were with the faculty. At first, the teachers and administrators met him with suspicion. Promises had been made before that were not kept, so they had no reason to believe his promises until they saw evidence. Nearly every Liberian would have taken a ticket out of the country to America if offered one, so naturally the Ricks personnel wondered why someone like Dr. Menjay came back when he didn't have to.

Slowly, the trust grew. With most of the teachers being older than Olu, many old enough to be his parents or grandparents, Dr. Menjay treated them with respect, calling them "Mr." and "Mrs." He listened to them and was patient. Yet he wasn't afraid to lead, hold teachers accountable, cast a vision, have high expectations, or share praise when projects were done well.

Just as the Apostle Paul had a base for his ministry, Dr. Menjay began to use his base of relationships in the States to help rebuild the school. In the process, he realized he was getting the opportunity to do what he had always wanted to do—teach missions. With every person and every team that travel to Ricks Institute, Dr. Menjay becomes the missiologist on the field. He knows well how culture, people groups, evangelism, pastoral care, and homiletics apply to missions. In addition, he is now an educator. He is still listening and learning about what it takes to raise math scores and reading levels within each age group of his school.

As Dr. Menjay made his way back into his old environment, he had to readjust to the lack of modern conveniences. He moved to a campus without electricity or running water. The only way he could initially get electricity into the house where he lived was to hook a power cord to the battery of the car he had borrowed. He didn't even have a bed, so he slept on the floor.

In going back to his home country where he wanted to teach missions, he found himself doing missions to all kinds of people—prostitutes; hungry and homeless people; those with diseases like malaria and HIV; illiterate and orphaned people; those traumatized by the flashbacks of a gruesome war; those who had lost hope or were losing hope; and people who were unsaved,

Two Ricks students drink from one of the wells on campus. Wells are shallow, and the warm temperatures allow bacteria to grow in the water. Safe drinking fountains purified by ultraviolet light and powered by solar energy have been installed on campus, gifts of the Woman's Missionary Union.

specifically those of the Islamic faith. In doing missions, Dr. Menjay found significance in his ministry. As James wrote (James 1:22a), "But be ye doers of the word, and not hearers only." Dr. Menjay's arrival at Ricks in 2005 changed his entire outlook on life. He let go of the American idea of success and replaced it with a desire to live a life of significance.

One of the first buildings to receive repairs after Dr. Menjay arrived was the auditorium. This room is large enough to hold the entire student population and faculty of more than 400 individuals. The morning chapel service and other meetings convene there. As workers repaired the ceiling of the auditorium, news came that a skilled carpenter's son, a Ricks student, had taken a serious fall on the playground, causing a severe spinal injury. He was rushed to the hospital that offers only basic (and poor) care.

A couple of days later, the carpenter came back to the school in his work clothes and gave Dr. Menjay the terrible news. With tears in his eyes, he said, "My son died."

Dr. Menjay replied, "I am so sorry, but what are you doing here? What can we do to help you?"

"I came to work so I can get paid. That's why I am here," the worker replied.

"No, no, no. You do not have to come to work. Please, please, you do not have to come to work." Dr. Menjay had money in his pocket and gave it to the man. The man needed the money to have the boy carried from the hospital to the morgue.

"When is the funeral?" Dr. Menjay asked.

The man replied that without the means to move the body from the morgue to the village for burial, he didn't know when the funeral would take place. Olu told him that he would see that the body was carried to the village for burial.

In America, we don't think much about the basic service we pay the funeral home to do—to drive our deceased loved ones to the burial site. In Liberia, there's no such service. Families are responsible for arranging the transport.

The next day, when Olu came to campus, the father and a group of his helpers were in the workshop building a casket from the discarded ceiling tiles of the auditorium. Olu could never have imagined that one of the first things he would do as principal of Ricks Institute would be to watch a casket being made of ceiling tiles from the auditorium of his school, and then to arrange the transport of a deceased student's body from the morgue to the grave site in the village.

New Opportunities

Bringing the World to Ricks

The significance of Olu's decision to return to Liberia is bearing fruit. Dr. Menjay is slowly bringing Ricks Institute into the twenty-first century with the hope of individuals, churches, and organizations who have partnered with the school to help educate Liberia's youth. With each repair, with each improvement, with each reached goal, the students at Ricks realize there are people in this world who care deeply for them, people who believe they are the hope of Liberia. The adults at Ricks are humbled that people choose to partner with them in the education of their children. The children and youth are excited when they realize people think of them, pray for them, and care enough about them to ensure they receive a quality education.

Dr. Menjay has opened the world to his students by bringing the Internet to his campus. Most of the students at Ricks have never traveled more than 60 miles from their homes. Until recently, most had never even seen water run freely from a faucet. Children are naïve about how the world

While Dr. Menjay opens Ricks to the world, cooking is still done in the most primitive of ways, on an earthen stove. The work is hot and laborious.

operates; one child thought airplanes flew on tracks. It's difficult for their minds to grow when they haven't even seen the possibilities that exist. None of these children own anything that uses electricity. Since most will never travel outside a third-world country, bringing the world to them through the Internet was a significant step in helping expand their worldview and enhance their research skills.

Dr. Menjay has also brought the world to Ricks by convincing several church groups and leaders to make the journey across the Atlantic to assist the Liberian school. Sonoraville Baptist Church in Calhoun, Georgia, did a beautiful job repairing the house on campus where Dr. Menjay first lived. They also made repairs to the guesthouse next door. First Baptist Church of Columbus, Georgia, repaired the girls' dormitory that had been occupied by refugees. First Baptist Church in Jonesboro, Georgia, repaired the boys' dormitory, which displaced people had also occupied. First Baptist Church of El Dorado, Kansas, sent a combined construction/medical/outreach team to Ricks and helped open the medical clinic. A work team from Trinity Baptist Church in Moultrie, Georgia, restored water to the main building, school cafeteria, and health clinic. This project was in partnership with the Moultrie Rotary Club, Milledge Avenue Baptist Church Foundation, and the Cooperative Baptist Fellowship of Georgia.

Dr. Richard F. Wilson, chairperson of Roberts Christianity Department of Mercer University, first visited Ricks Institute in March 2007. After his visit, consultation with Dr. Menjay, and assessment of the work done at Ricks, he decided to make the school one of the sites for Mercer University's Mercer on Mission Program. The four-week, study-abroad program is the dream of President William D. Underwood. Its uniqueness combines study with service in a cross-cultural setting. The goal of the program is to transform lives by transforming minds through rigorous study, transform hearts through meaningful service, and transform souls through spiritual reflection.

Although the Mercer on Mission program transforms lives in Liberia, the lives of the Mercer students are similarly transformed. College students are entering an increasingly materialistic world. Pursuing a financial goal of owning more "stuff" reflects a general cultural trend toward materialism. A 1970 survey of about a quarter-million new college students found that 40 percent considered "being very well-off financially" to be important, and about 70 percent considered "developing a meaningful philosophy of life" to be important. By 1987, and continuing through the most recent survey, these numbers reversed. In 2005, about 70 percent of entering college students considered being well-off financially as important, while about 40 percent considered developing a meaningful philosophy of life very important.[2]

President Underwood's Mercer on Mission program is giving students an opportunity to look at life through a different lens. As a result, the students who come to Liberia wrestle with tough questions: How can a country in the twenty-first century exist without electricity? How is it possible for the capitol building in Monrovia to operate without running water? How does a country exist with only three physicians? (The number may be greater now.) How could one in every ten people in the country die in a fourteen-year civil war? Where is the justice? Where is the mercy? The Mercer on Mission program profoundly affects not just the students of Ricks and the people of Liberia, but the lives (and attitudes) of the students who participate.

The Gift of a Laptop

After spending three weeks at Ricks in March/April 2006, I left my Gateway laptop computer as a gift to the school. Dr. Menjay gave the computer to Mr. Varney Sherman, academic supervisor at Ricks. Mr. Sherman had never owned nor used a computer in his life. With no one to assist him, he taught himself how to use all the programs on the computer.

Dr. Menjay was in Prague, Czech Republic, when invitations went out in July for the 2007–2008 closing convocation. Olu didn't receive an advance copy of the invitation to proof, nor did he see the finalized invitation list. Mr. Sherman did all the work, preparing the invitations on a program he'd taught himself to use on the laptop computer.

Meg Regg, public diplomacy officer at the United States Embassy, received one of the invitations; Mr. Sherman also sent her an analysis of the school's academic records for the year. Meg attended the commencement ceremony at Ricks. In conversation with her, Dr. Menjay commended Mr. Sherman's work and told her that Sherman made the attractive invitation and prepared the school's analysis after teaching himself how to use the programs on the laptop computer.

Meg was impressed. She told Dr. Menjay that she needed a teacher from Liberia to send to the United States to study through the International Visitor Program sponsored by the State Department. She asked Dr. Menjay if he thought Mr. Sherman would be a good candidate. With a wide smile of hope, Dr. Menjay said, "I think he would be a great choice."

Mr. Sherman left Liberia on September 15, 2008. Along with several educators from around Africa, he spent time learning about various secondary schools around the United States. The goal of the program was to introduce participants to the dynamics of secondary education in the United States. They traveled to seven different states and several dozen schools during this visit. They were able to take in a show on Broadway in New York City and tour Washington, D.C.

A week before his return to Liberia in October, Dr. Menjay arranged for Mr. Sherman to spend a week in Columbus, Georgia, at the Brookstone School. He used that time to familiarize himself with that school, which happens to be the sister school of Ricks Institute.

Dr. Richard F. Wilson, one of Menjay's former professors at Mercer and leader of the first Mercer on Mission program to Ricks, invited Mr. Sherman to visit with President Underwood at Mercer University. Since Mercer on Mission began a partnership with the school in 2008, President Underwood has shown a strong interest in the disadvantaged countries of the world and a particular interest in Liberia and Ricks Institute. Before the meeting concluded, President Underwood made a commitment to Mr. Sherman that, beginning with the 2008–2009 graduating class, Mercer would provide two scholarships for the two most deserving persons in the Ricks community. In August 2009, Edmond Cooper, 2008 valedictorian at Ricks, and James Blay, student affairs coordinator from 2005–2009, became the first recipients of the president's scholarship.

When I heard this story, I smiled, thinking that it all began with a donated laptop. What separates the literate from the illiterate, the poor from those who can provide for themselves, is rarely ability; it is opportunity.

Whenever we give, our gifts come back tenfold and a hundred fold. President Underwood will touch thousands of lives because of his investment in giving a few Liberian individuals the opportunity for an education they would not have otherwise. He will change their lives and others' lives forever.

Dr. Menjay's love for the students is evident. He stands with Kojo Achampong, one of the youngest members of the school.

When Dr. Menjay stepped onto the campus of Ricks Institute in 2005 and decided to focus on living a life of significance, he had no way of knowing that within three years God would send students and faculty from Mercer University to study and work with him in a cross-cultural setting, or that one of the Ricks faculty would travel to the States. Dr. Menjay has opportunities to help students answer significant questions that rise to the surface in programs of this nature: "What do I want to do in life? After I'm gone, what impact did I have?"

One of the greatest feelings in the world is to walk in the daily assurance that we are going to a job and living a life that is of consequence, that is significant. In the end, history may not remember our names. What we do and accomplish in this life will likely not be remembered beyond a generation or two. We will not likely accumulate great wealth or fame.

Even if we do, we must remember that someone else will one day own our earthly wealth. Fame is fleeting. However, if we store up for ourselves "treasures in heaven, where moth and rust do not destroy, and where thieves do not break in and steal" (Matt 6:20), then by God's grace, when we enter the gates of heaven we will hear the Master say, "Well done, good and faithful servant!" (Matt 25:23). Then we will know once and for all that we have lived a life of significance.

Notes

1. While it may sound rather formal to refer to my friend Olu as "Rev. Menjay" or "Dr. Olu Menjay," titles in Africa are important, as they are in the Black culture in America. Perhaps because life in Liberia was so devalued during the civil war, there is something refreshing about the level of respect Liberians are beginning to show one another. Respect is shown not only in how people address Dr. Menjay, but also in how he addresses others. For example, he addresses all of his faculty as "Mr." and "Mrs.," regardless of their age or position.

2. Dan N. Stone, Ben Wier, and Stephanie M. Bryant, "Reducing Materialism Through Financial Literacy," *The CPA Journal Online* 78/2 (February 2008): http://www.nysscpa.org/cpajournal/2008/208/perspectives/p12.htm.

Chapter 12

Reflecting on the Lessons and People of Liberia

Great Need vs. Great Abundance

In a place like Liberia, great needs abound. The children and teenagers at Ricks Institute, like many students in America, wear uniforms to school: light blue shirts, dark blue pants, and black shoes for the boys; blue dresses with dark blue collars and black shoes for the girls. Everybody looks the same. No one has to come to school ashamed of their clothing.

At first glance, their needs are barely noticeable. But when I saw where some of the children live, with seven people sleeping in one bed in a ten-by-ten-foot hut, I got a better picture of what real life is like for Liberians. When I saw that they cook every meal over an open fire and draw every drink of impure water from an open well, then I recognized the challenges they face every day.

My time in Liberia has made me keenly aware of what I consume and what I throw away. The richest fifth of the world's population

A mother and her son enjoy an evening meal, perhaps the only one of the day, in the internal displacement camp on the campus of Ricks Institute.

Classmates head home after a day at school.

consumes 86 percent of all goods and services and produces 53 percent of all carbon dioxide emissions, while the poorest fifth consumes 1.3 percent of goods and services and accounts for 3 percent of carbon dioxide output. That can only change as each person begins to think of the difference one life makes, how we live, what we consume, and what we throw away.[1]

In his book, *A Life on the Road,* Charles Kuralt tells about spending a day with a man who claimed to be the owner of the world's largest ball of string. During the entire interview, the man kept adding to his ball of string. Kuralt writes, "That's the trouble with owning the world's largest ball of string; you live in constant fear that somebody, somewhere is making a larger ball of string."[2]

I think it's the same way with those of us who get caught up in the race of acquiring things. We work hard to acquire what we have. Then we spend much of our time trying to keep what we have. Instead of *having* possessions, we allow our possessions to *have* us. For many people, the driving force in life becomes the things money buys, then the work required to continue to buy more things and keep up with the things we've already bought.

Scripture teaches us that the driving force in our lives should be God and the indwelling of God's Spirit. All aspects of our lives should revolve around God, including our money. When we refuse to acknowledge that God is the source of what we have, we allow what we have to become more important than God. When God takes a back seat to material things, we commit idolatry.

My trips to Liberia have helped me become a less material person. I'm not where I need to be, but I've learned to get by with less. These trips have reminded me that everything I own will one day belong to someone else—my car, my money, my clothes, my books, and my house. I'm merely a steward, temporarily taking care of and managing what's been given to me for a short time.

A non-boarding school child can be educated for an entire year at Ricks Institute for $400. Supplies like backpacks and lunchboxes come from sponsoring churches.

The Power of Relationships

As of November 2008, dozens of organizations and generous churches have joined in assisting Ricks Institute since Olu arrived as principal.[3] These partnerships show the forces behind the hope people are placing in the students and faculty of Ricks Institute.

Some of these organizations gave assistance in restoring the dormitories that allowed the school to function again as a boarding school. A boarding school in Liberia

1. eliminates transportation issues, as most children must otherwise walk to school.
2. ensures that the students' nutritional needs are met, as most students come from home hungry. Boarding school students are fed three meals a day.
3. ensures the student drinks purified water. Water on the Ricks campus is purified, while water in the surrounding villages is not 100 percent safe.
4. allows students more time each day to study. If students go home, many must do family chores. When the sun goes down, there is no light to study by, so students accomplish little homework. At school, they have more study hours.
5. allows for a child to attend school from a long distance away. The boarding school gives Ricks an opportunity to attract some of the brightest students from around the country, a feature the school was once known for. So far, the school educates students only in the Virginia, Liberia, area.

Some of the supporting organizations, along with friends of the school, participate in the Ricks Institute Student Sponsorship (RISS) program. With the help of these partners, Dr. Menjay was able to launch free primary education for students from kindergarten to grade six (more than 250 students), the first nongovernmental school in Liberia to launch such a program. At the launching ceremony, U.S. Ambassador to Liberia Donald Booth commended Dr. Menjay for leading the way to the free primary education initiative in Liberia. In a country where the average Liberian lives on thirty cents a day and half the country's children do not attend school, such an action is significant.

Parents or guardians of the children who benefit from the program are required to volunteer at the school three hours per month in whatever area they feel comfortable. Some parents or guardians spend time in the classroom with their kids, while others volunteer in the library and the dining hall. The free quality educational initiative is intended to go on for the next four years with the hope that the socioeconomic situation in Liberia will improve to the point where families can afford to pay for their children's education.

In 2008, Christine Barber, a fifth grader at R. B. Wright School in Moultrie, Georgia, became a pen pal with Maima Grant, a fourth grader at Ricks Institute. Christine's family paid for Maima's education through the RISS program during the 2007–2008 school term. Maima sent the family her report card from the end of the school year. She had an 86.3 average for the year. In April 2008, she wrote,

An older student sits with a child during a chapel service at Ricks.

Dear Christine:

It takes me a great pleasure and opportunity to compose you this few words. My reason is that I will like to give you and your family the appreciation for what you are doing for me and also the school principal and his instructors; for the knowledge that they are giving me in school to stand among peoples, to show them that the school called Ricks Institute is not a small school. I pray for them to carry on their good job and also I pray for you sis, Christine.

Maima

Such relationships are significant. Two children separated by race, culture, economics, and opportunities are joined by a common desire for education, love, and friendship.

In December 2007, Liberian president Ellen Johnson-Sirleaf made an impromptu visit to Ricks Institute. She praised the administration for fostering an excellent educational vision for Liberian children and challenged

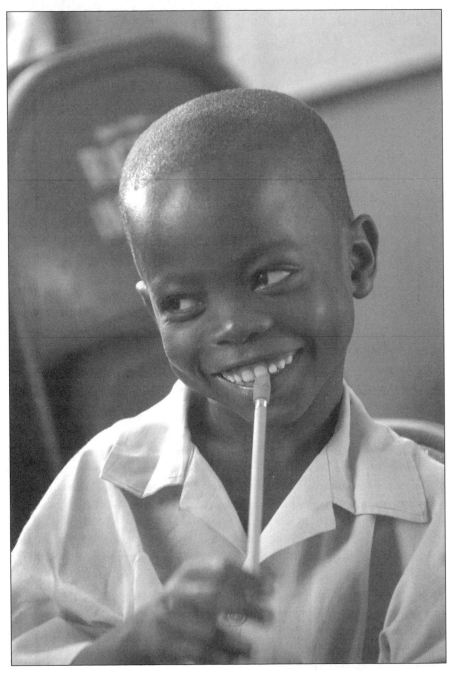

A smile spreads across Darlington Beyslow's face during chapel service.
No pencil, paper, or books are taken for granted by Ricks students.

students to study hard in becoming good citizens and servant leaders in Liberia. Her visit was a significant affirmation and encouragement for faculty and students.

Other organizations have gotten involved with the school's mission. The Cooperative Baptist Fellowship (CBF) in partnership with First Baptist Church Columbus, Georgia, bought the first large generator for the school, the same one that now provides electricity for the campus.

Jade and Shelah Acker, CBF field workers in West Africa, conducted a workshop on HIV/AIDS at Ricks. They also helped improve Bible curriculum for instruction.

Through the Woman's Missionary Union's (WMU) "Project MOST" Program, people can purchase livestock for children at Ricks Institute. "Most" is the Croatian word for bridge. Through "Project MOST," WMU not only bridges two parts of the world, but also helps create bridges of opportunity for others. Through this program, children receive immediate benefits of the animal (e.g., milk or meat from the offspring). They also learn animal husbandry skills, enabling their families to earn a living. A gift to the International Initiatives Fund of the WMU, designated for Ricks Institute, can help provide a goat for $100, a pig for $75, or chickens for $1 each. This program affected Ricks ninth grader Jacob (2008–2009). Jacob wants to become an agriculturist. He believes it's time for Liberians to use their God-given abilities to feed themselves. Jacob feeds the pigs daily and bathes them on Saturdays at the piggery located on campus. He is learning skills that will help sustain him later in life.

The Pure Water Pure Love program of the WMU provided a grant used to purchase solar purification systems, which provide bacteria-free drinking water for the students. Water passes through an ultraviolet light, powered by solar panels placed on the roof of the school. The ultraviolet light kills all germs in the water.

Passport Camps, based in Birmingham, Alabama, and headed by David Burrough, provided a $34,000 gift to purchase the first solar energy power solution for the academic building. The gift was made possible by offerings given by youth during Passport Camps in the United States. These youth brought hope to Ricks through the gift of electricity, which provided much-needed lighting and power to run computers and other equipment for the administrative and academic buildings at Ricks. Because of this gift, the basement area was opened for additional classrooms, allowing the school to increase enrollment.

Sometimes the best ideas are born from the interest of students. When sixth grade students from Brookstone School in Columbus, Georgia, began pen pal relationships with students from Ricks Institute, the teachers and administrators noted the high level of interest. They got creative. Through the miracle of technology, a series of digital video conferences was set up in October 2006. Through these conferences, the students began to learn the differences in each other's cultures.

The video conference in Liberia was held at the United States Embassy, while Brookstone had access to this technology at their school. In one poignant moment, the students of each school were asked, "Do you agree with the war in Iraq?" Almost all of the American students' hands were raised. None of the Liberian students' hands were raised. The difference? The Liberian students had seen and lived with war. They knew war from a different perspective. They might not have understood all the issues of the Iraq war, but they knew that people, even innocent people, were being killed in Iraq. To them, that was the difference.

Scott Wilson, headmaster of Brookstone School, and Principal Menjay were both enthusiastic and excited over their newfound relationship. Following this series of video conferences, Headmaster Wilson decided that Brookstone School would offer to host two students from Ricks Institute at the beginning of the 2007 school year for four months. I was on campus at Ricks Institute in April 2006 when it was announced that Bendu Sherman and Isatta Musahson were the faculty's choices for the high honor.

It's difficult to explain the huge learning curve in culture these girls experienced. They had never used anything electrical. They had never been to an airport or watched television. They had never eaten at a restaurant or been to a department store. Unless it was eaten fresh, most everything they had eaten was cooked over an open fire.

Every day was a learning experience for these young ladies. In America, they drank their first glass of cold milk and had their first bowl of cereal. They had to acquire a taste for sweets, as their diets in Liberia mostly consisted of rice and a starchy vegetable. They ate their first sandwiches. Before they returned to Liberia, they had acquired a taste for Chick-fil-A. Once, they thought the house would catch on fire when a bag of popcorn popped in the microwave.

In spite of the girls' naiveté regarding the modern world, host mom Tammy Gorum was surprised at their maturity. "There's a kind of confidence that comes from all they've been through," she said.

In a similar program in fall 2008, Alfreda Brewer, a ninth grader, was given the opportunity to study at Oak Hill Academy, a Baptist boarding school in Mouth of Wilson, Virginia.

Dr. Menjay hopes his students return from these experiences with confidence, added knowledge, and a greater ability and desire to lead. He wants their world to expand. He wants them to know the possibilities that are within the reach of their own country. Perhaps one of these girls will study at Harvard and be the next Ellen Johnson-Sirleaf. Liberia needs educated young people who understand the world in order for the country to reach its potential.

Ricks Institute is being rebuilt on relationships with Baptists and other Christians. This is the foundation on which the school was originally built. It was sustained by such efforts in its early years until the school began accepting money from the Liberian government. The money from the Liberian government was actually a reward for the good work of the school. Free money is hard to turn down. It was put to good use, but accepting the government money turned out to be a mistake. For many years, the Southern Baptist Convention provided missionaries and money for Ricks. When Ricks began accepting funds from the government, however, the convention ceased the relationship with the school, citing a

Uniforms worn by nearly all school children in Liberia help to hide their poverty.

conflict of interest over the issue of separation of church and state. When the relationship with Southern Baptists ended, the Liberian Missionary and Education Convention did not fill the monetary gap, as Liberia had fallen on hard economic times.

The Southern Baptist missionary influence in Liberia was monumental, but eventually, all Southern Baptist missionaries left the country. Many Liberian Baptists feel that Southern Baptists left them when they needed missionaries the most. The school and churches were left to suffer at a time in history when they desperately needed help.

The good work the missionaries did at Ricks Institute, and throughout the country, is still evident today. In fact, with the presence of Dr. Menjay at Ricks, their efforts have come full circle. Dr. Menjay, baptized by a Southern Baptist missionary as a boy, has now returned as the principal on a campus once supported by gifts from Southern Baptists.

There's more than one way to win people to Jesus, and there's more than one kind of effective evangelism. There's more than one way to be missional. Being evangelistic involves more than just the telling. We used to send missionaries who did a lot more "doing of the word." Missionaries used to win the right to be heard before they ever preached. They used to dig wells, plant seeds, drive nails, serve as teachers and administrators, teach home economics, and heal bodies. Many missionaries met the physical needs of the people before they introduced them to the Savior. This is the kind of missions Olu Menjay grew up learning in Liberia. It's missions right out of the book of James:

> What good is it, my brothers, if a man claims to have faith but has no deeds? Can such faith save him? Suppose a brother or sister is without clothes and daily food. If one of you says to him, "Go, I wish you well; keep warm and well fed," but does nothing about his physical needs, what good is it? In the same way, faith by itself, if it is not accompanied by action, is dead. (Jas 2:14-17 NIV)

Where do you suppose James learned this? I think he learned it from his brother Jesus. I think after seeing Jesus minister to people in this way time after time after time, James got the message.

"Be Careful with Your Camera"

The lives of photojournalists have always fascinated me. Given the chance to choose another career in another life, perhaps I would travel the world, capture pictures of people in their own environments, and share their stories. Yet I realize the lives of photojournalists are far from glamorous. Getting publishable photographs and a story requires sacrifice and dedication that sometimes places them in dangerous and compromising situations. Their job requires great imagination and creativity as well as the skill and knowledge of two trades.

During my first trip to Monrovia in 1995, I carried my camera with me everywhere. There was one problem: I wasn't free to use it openly. Because Liberia is a war-torn country, people who were once open and friendly to outsiders have turned inward and become paranoid. "Someone might mistake your innocent photograph as a hostile action, so be careful

Amid growing foliage, this sign reminds Liberians violence quickly grows from small to large groups.

with your camera," I was told. Although I wanted to take photos, I complied and kept my camera out of sight most of the time. But many sights—buildings, natural scenery, and people—made me wish I could use it more often.

On most days during the ten-day trip, I preached at the historic Providence Baptist Church, which has a large sanctuary with beautiful stained-glass windows. The evening before his assassination, President William Tolbert had attended a choir concert at the Centennial Pavilion adjacent to Providence Baptist.

The original stone sanctuary was built in 1839. Within that structure, the nation of Liberia, Africa's first independent nation, was born. The first Legislative Assembly, consisting of the House of Representatives and the Senate, met there. Because of this, Providence Baptist is revered as "The Cornerstone of the Nation." I was privileged to preach within the historic walls of that stone sanctuary. Providence Baptist also hosted the YouthChallenge Liberia conference, and I trained workers in youth ministry there.

Special revival services were held each day of the week in the middle of the afternoon, as there were no lights for an evening church, nor could people safely travel after dark due to the potential for violence. With the exception of those who drove me to the church, everyone who came to the worship service arrived on foot. The crowds were modest but faithful. Mrs. Gracie A. Davis, a nurse in her sixties, attended each day dressed in her white nursing uniform. She worked at the John F. Kennedy Hospital about five miles away. Although she worked faithfully six days a week, she had not received payment in six months. Because of the war, the economic system was broken, and people who worked for government or public agencies could not be paid. She continued to work out of loyalty, compassion for the patients, and the hope that she would eventually receive her wages.

Michael Vernon, a young blind man, came each day with his African drum. He teamed up with Mrs. Davis, who shook the salsa, and together they provided the rhythm for our singing. Michael reminded me of a Liberian Stevie Wonder. He smiled often and moved his head from side to side as he stroked the drum. He obviously found great joy in using his talent.

Months after I returned to the States, I received a letter from Michael, with the following request: "I am a blind student, a high school graduate whose ambition is to pursue education at the highest possible level. I also desire to know more about the Holy Scriptures. I am therefore making an appeal through this medium for a Bible and Bible study materials designed especially for the blind. Thanks for your kind attention to my letter and may God bless us all. Yours in Christ, Michael Vernon." I secured a Braille Bible and shipped it to Liberia.

The last day I preached at Providence Baptist, I hoped to take a few good pictures of the church. As I stood ready to snap a photo of the huge banner hanging in front of the church to announce the revival, a young Liberian woman walked by carrying a large bowl of plantain on her head, the typical way Liberians carry most of their items. I asked her if I could take her picture. With a bit of shyness, she agreed.

Children carry freshly harvested plantain home to share with their family.

After I took only one shot of the young lady, I heard a man yelling from across the street, "Excuse me! Excuse me! You took my photo without permission! You took my photo!" As he made his way toward me, his voice grew louder, making it clear that he was angry.

I explained that I had not taken his photo. As our disagreement continued, he became louder and more animated. This drew the attention of my friends. By the time they arrived, I was ready to give the man five dollars to go away, figuring he wanted money, but my friends objected. One friend pulled me to the side and explained, "There are still many criminals on the streets who fear that if their photo is taken, they might be identified."

The man overheard my friend and angrily claimed that my friend had called him "a criminal," which my friend denied. They got into an argument. By this time about thirty people had encircled us, drawing the attention of a couple of policemen. The arguing, which continued about ten minutes, finally drew the attention of the pastor of Providence Baptist. The pastor arrived and suggested we take the discussion off the street and inside the church as the crowds continued to gather.

I was embarrassed. How could my taking a simple photograph escalate into such a confrontation? But I was in another culture and needed to abide by another country's laws. As we entered the church, I nervously wondered what would happen.

A heated Liberian discussion is an interesting cultural experience. It's animated, loud, and passionate. This group seemed to make a real effort to understand the truth. I remained quiet through about twenty minutes of the discussion. Finally, I asked if I could speak.

At that time, I was using the 35mm Minolta x-700 camera that I had owned since my days in college. It occurred to me that I could solve the whole issue by volunteering to give up my roll of film. I was willing to sacrifice the photos to help resolve the problem. This caught my accuser off guard and was obviously not what he wanted. He objected and began to give his reasons why that wouldn't suffice.

At that point, the two policemen abruptly stood up and ordered the man to the back room. The pastor also left the room with the men. When they returned, one of the policemen said, "Our brother has decided to forgive you." The room filled with laughter. Everyone knew then his true motives. "He has decided to forgive you" was an interesting way to save face. We shook hands, did the Liberian finger snap (as Liberians shake hands they snap their middle fingers together as they release the handshake), and all went our separate ways. Everyone in my party laughed and gave me a hard time for the rest of the trip. "So, Michael, you want to take some more photos today?" they asked each day.

At the end of my trip as we gathered at the Liberian Baptist Theological Seminary, I received several parting gifts. The group recalled how Michael Vernon, the blind drummer, had captivated me, and they recalled how much controversy one photo had caused outside Providence Baptist Church. I was given two authentic Liberian carvings. One was a wooden carving of a Liberian man playing the drum, and the other was a carving of a typical Liberian woman carrying a wooden bowl on her head.

Those two carvings are treasures to me. When I see them, I sometimes sit and think about the people they represent, but mostly I think about the thoughtful people who gave them to me. At a time when people struggled to put food on the table, they pooled money to purchase thoughtful gifts for me as I left the country.

When I reviewed the photographs I took during the trip, as expected, I had not taken a photo of the man across the street. The picture of the young girl carrying her bowl of plantain will always evoke special memories. The roll of film contained photos that represent hope and suffering. A picture of a light pole with broken power lines signifies the country's hardship because the war destroyed all electrical service in the country. Another shows two boys with their father, one boy holding a homemade slingshot in his hand and the other holding a tiny bird he had caught and claimed for a pet. Their play is a sign of hope that they could at least temporarily escape the fear of war. Unfortunately, neither of these boys will know a peaceful childhood.

Ricks students assemble for the flag-raising ceremony prior to morning chapel.

Photographs of Students with a Future: Virginia, Liberia, 2006

With hope returning to Liberia and with Rev. Menjay's efforts to reestablish Ricks Institute as a viable boarding school, I traveled to Liberia in April 2006 for a one-month sabbatical on my tenth anniversary as pastor of Trinity Baptist Church in Moultrie, Georgia. Rev. Menjay invited me to stay in the renovated guesthouse and serve as the school's first guest pastor. He assured me I would have adequate time to read, rest, reflect, pray, and study. He also told me that my time with students and teachers would be stimulating and challenging as they shared about their lives and their experiences of living through the civil war.

Each morning at Ricks, school begins with an opening assembly. One of the upperclassmen leads the school in a cheerful song. This is followed by devotion and sometimes a challenge from the principal that sets the tone for the remainder of the school day. During my month at Ricks, my devotions focused on aspects of character such as honesty, faithfulness, loyalty, kindness, and self-control.

Although the devotions were a major focus each morning, what gave me the most joy was playing the role of school photographer. Each morning after recess, a different class joined me in the library so I could take individual school photos. I had never taken school pictures before, but I'd been on the other side of the lens enough that I figured I'd do a decent job. A teacher gave me a tie-dyed tablecloth, which I used as a backdrop. With my own makeshift photo studio set up, I was in business. For these students, it was the first time they had ever had their picture taken in a school uniform. It was the first time in the school's history that school pictures had ever been taken!

I had shipped six hundred pages of photo paper, my Canon i860 printer, and printer ink ahead in a container that arrived several months before I did. I carried my laptop computer (which I left behind as a gift) along with my digital Nikon D-2H camera and tripod for picture taking and downloading. Each day when I returned to my guest quarters, I downloaded the digital photos to my computer and printed out a photo package for the students to carry home to their families. Each evening, a generator run by the ECOMOG troops who maintained a base on the campus provided the electricity I needed to run my equipment.

Each morning I posted the pictures on the board after the chapel service. I also put together a class collage for the entire school to view. The students' first opportunity to see the pictures came during their lunch break. Every day, they ran during lunch to the display board, where each student's picture hung. These hungry children ran to the board before heading to the lunch area.

During my time at Ricks, I began to carry my camera with me into the refugee camp. I won the people over by asking if I could take pictures of the children playing soccer. My digital camera takes eight shots per second. After one boy kicked the ball through the goal, I'd taken about twelve pictures. I turned the camera around for other children to see as the camera displayed the action right before their eyes, frame by frame. It was like magic. All the children in the camp wanted to kick the ball and have me take their pictures. Even adults wanted me to take their pictures and have me turn the camera around so they could see themselves.

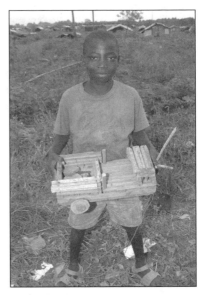

A child in the internal displacement camp on the Ricks campus proudly displays one of his toys. The only toys children have are homemade.

The real surprise came the day I walked into the refugee camp with actual printed photographs of people in the camp. I felt like Santa Claus handing out gifts from his big red bag. The children came to know me as "white man." Children would run out from inside their huts and say, "Hey, white man. Take my picture, white man."

Unfortunately, the pictures hurt my heart. These refugee children were the poorest of the poor. A few of them actually went to school at Ricks. The children of Miatta, one of the school cooks, attended classes. Since Miatta worked for the school, her children attended for free. Most of the other children in the camp,

Teenagers attend Ricks with dreams of finishing school and continuing their education at schools of higher learning. Opportunities for advanced learning are rare.

however, were unable to attend school. They were growing up as part of a large group of illiterate children within the nation.

As I took the class pictures of Ricks students, I noted the differences between photos of younger and older children. It was easy to get the youngest children to smile. The older the grades, the more serious the children became when they sat for their photos. They joked and had fun up until the point of sitting for their pictures, but actually having the photographs taken became a serious matter.

Regardless of what that meant culturally, it was a fitting metaphor for what they had endured in life. The younger children were freer, more at ease, smiling more easily. The older children had experienced more trauma and had missed out on childhood. It was harder to catch them in the act of smiling. They are all seriously composed in the photographs, especially the seniors.

In any school, seniors are a special group. Perhaps I was drawn to that class because my son John was a senior at the time. Maybe it was because I knew some of their riveting and heartbreaking stories. One of the seniors, Morris Kamara, was left orphaned from the war. He was fourteen when he and his family were taken before a rebel leader named "Kill the Bitch." "Kill the Bitch" was seated beside a fence and surrounded by more than ten dead people whom he had just killed. This man was covered in blood, and Morris described him as "having the appearance of the Devil himself."

After seeking the origin of Morris's family, the rebel leader accused Mr. Kamara and his family of being kin to the late President Doe. They were not related, and Morris's father denied it when accused. The rebel leader asked if anyone could identify whether the family were Krahn people or Kpelleh. No one could.

"Kill the Bitch" called Morris's two-year-old brother forward and asked, "Tell me the truth. You people are Krahn, right?"

Morris's little brother, obviously afraid of the man, answered, "Yes."

"Kill the Bitch" accused Mr. Kamara of being a liar. He ordered that Morris's mother be raped repeatedly while the family watched. She had delivered a child only a week before. The family was forced to laugh about the rape. Mrs. Kamara died from the repeated raping. Then "Kill the Bitch" ordered the rebels to shoot the family. All the family members were shot in the head, including Morris. The bullet grazed his skull, knocking him out. He awoke sometime later. The rebels were gone, but his entire family was dead.

Then there was Mustafa Flomo (not his real name), a senior captured by the National Patriotic Front of Liberia (NPFL) on the Ricks Institute campus when he was thirteen years old. Mustafa represented thousands of boys who were forced into fighting during the war. More than 500 people of his community were killed, including many from his family. The commanders forced him to take drugs to overcome the fear of being killed and the shock of witnessing death up close on the battlefield and to mask the stain that killing leaves on the human soul. Mustafa still wakes up at night crying out in his sleep because he sees images of the rebels who took him and forced him to fight. He still sees pictures of the fighting on the front lines. Yet he is comforted by the belief that God has a purpose for his life. "I know that God has something for me in this life," he says. "One day I believe God will manifest it to me."

When Bobby Brown sat down for his photo, I thought about the conversations we had after school. I later went back and reviewed what he wrote for the essay contest I sponsored. Bobby wrote,

> I learned from the Liberian civil war that prolonged violence brings about untold suffering and leads to the unwanted destruction of lives and property; that power-greedy politicians or warlords used innocent civilians as scapegoats to accomplish their selfish aim; that malice, hatred, destructive jealousy, and greed were used to acquire quick wealth or prosperity. While the rule of law was broken down, jungle justice was on the rampage. No amount of lawlessness is a solution to the problem. As a people we need to do away with personal sentiments and live within the confines of the law. I also learned that the culture of impurity is a major contributing factor to the Liberian civil conflict; that all Liberians should unite with one love, irrespective of background, creed, or tribe in order to forge ahead.

As I took their photographs, the senior boys took turns swapping ties. A dark blue tie is the one distinguishing piece of clothing that separates senior males from underclassmen. With not enough ties to go around, they shared with each other during the photo shoot.

When it came to photographing the senior girls, I noticed that they were not so different from American girls. They all wanted to look picture perfect. Without compact cases and mirrors for last-minute touchups, they relied on each other for help.

As Thomastina posed, I thought about her story, not uncommon among this class. She had an uncle and a grandfather killed in the war. She had a brother who was captured by the NPFL and forced to fight for the rebels.

When she was seven years old, she was walking with her parents from Paynesville Police Academy to Clara Town in Bushrod Island when a rebel soldier killed a man her father's age before her eyes. She remembers hiding behind a bush and watching as the man fought to remain alive, slowly losing the fight until all life had drained away from him.

After learning what these young men and women had been through, I was honored to take their pictures. I was proud of them for their progress. I was hopeful for what they might yet accomplish in spite of the many obstacles ahead of them.

I thought about the high school dropout rate in America. More than a million teenagers drop out of high school every year in a country that offers free education and endless opportunities for the educated. What a difference to leave America and go to a country where students must pay for an education, where there are not enough schools, teachers, or money to pay the tuition of students who want to attend. While I was in Liberia, several children asked me if I would help them attend school by paying their school fees.

As I took photographs of the senior class, I wished I could have brought each teenager who had dropped out of my local high school to meet them. These students from Ricks Institute chose to graduate from high school even though the unemployment rate in Liberia is around 85 percent. Even though there are few jobs, these young people hope that an education will help turn their country around.

These students are survivors in a land where they lost their innocence early in life. The war took away their childhood. Many lost parents and family members in the fighting. They were displaced from their homes more than once. Rebel soldiers invaded their campus. Some of the graduating seniors were forced to fight as boy soldiers. Most went home each day to illiterate parents. When they went home, they had to study by the sunlight or by candlelight. Some of them were more than twenty years old when they received their diplomas. However, they were determined.

These students learned that there is a high price to pay for ignorance. Varney Gballey, an eleventh grader, summed it up well:

> I'm emphasizing education because we all know it was illiteracy that caused most Liberians to embrace the genesis of such bloody rebellion that caused many to lose their precious lives and millions of dollars of damaged property, thereby leading us to be behind in the world. I hope that President Sirleaf will

turn her 85 percent illiterate population into a literate people by constructing vocational schools, more high schools and universities in the various counties.

Varney is right. A nation is vulnerable any time her people are uneducated. Liberia's people were easily led astray because they were illiterate and uneducated.

The picture-taking experience meant more than I ever expected. I wanted to give the students and their parents a gift. I imagined how much joy and surprise the families would experience as their children brought home a packet of school pictures, the only school photographs the family had ever owned.

However, I underestimated the deeper meaning of what the experience meant to the school. Principal Menjay said, "Taking the photographs made an important statement. It said, 'We are no longer survivors but a people with a future.' We can take pictures knowing we have a future. One day the students will look at these pictures with the memory of being in grade school and high school."

The senior class of 2006 will look back one day at their senior pictures, remembering that they graduated from high school in spite of a war that took so much from them. Not only did they survive, but they are people with a future. Praise God; the war did not take away their hope for a future! That's what a diploma meant to the senior class of 2006. They are people with a future.

A Lesson from the Chickens

One evening, I followed a path back to the guesthouse on the campus of Ricks Institute in Virginia, Liberia. I passed the residence of Charles Wiah. He sat outside in a straight-backed chair along with Miss Monen Duoe, the new first grade teacher of Ricks Institute, who was slicing plantain while warming vegetable oil in a pot over coals.

"Have you ever had any fried plantain chips?" Mr. Wiah asked.

"No, I never have," I said. "Is this what I see some of the children bringing to school in a bucket to sell during recess?"

"Yes, it is," said Miss Duoe.

"Well, have a seat. Be my guest. We will fry you up a bowl of plantain," said Mr. Wiah.

Plantain looks like a banana but doesn't turn as yellow. When deep fried, the fruit becomes crisp like a potato chip.

The sun in the western sky at Ricks Institute.

As we sat and got to know one another, the chickens and ducks wandered freely around the grass-free back yard. My mind flashed back to my childhood when chickens roamed our yard and always made their way back to the chicken house at dusk to roost on posts that ran horizontally at different levels. Those posts were smooth from being gripped through the years by chickens' feet. I always wondered how the birds managed to sleep standing up. I wondered if any ever fell off the roost during the night.

Mr. Wiah told me that sometimes when it's quiet at sunset, he sits and thinks about the mysteries of God. "Once I was sitting here as the chickens were gathering for the evening," he said, "and I watched a hen spread out her wings to gather in all her little chicks. As soon as she settled down over them, she knew something was not right. She rose up and immediately started pecking on a few chicks because she knew they were not hers. They had mistakenly gotten mixed in with her chicks, and she knew it right away. Now what is it, do you suppose, that God put into that chicken to make her realize just by the touch of her wings that some of those chicks were not hers?"

Then he directed my attention to the individual baskets on the ground where

Nothing is wasted. I was amused that boxes donated by the Mobley Plant Company to ship books and supplies had become the evening roost of a hen and her chicks.

the chickens returned to roost during the evening. In addition to the handmade baskets, a Mobley Plant Company box was used as a roosting box. The Mobleys own a plant company in Moultrie, Georgia. Months before my arrival, a container with hundreds of boxes of tools, books, food, and supplies from our church arrived at the school. Many of those items were stored in boxes donated by Mobley Plant Company. I'm sure the Mobleys never imagined that one of their boxes would become home to a Liberian hen and her newly hatched chicks. Nothing of value is wasted in Liberia.

Mr. Wiah pointed out that the chickens fan out all over the campus during the day. But during the evening, all the chickens know their way back home. In addition, each chicken knows its individual basket or box.

While the plantain chips fried in the vegetable oil, I watched with amusement as the chicks followed the mother hens into their individual baskets. Once the chickens and chicks were settled, Mr. Wiah's children came out, closed up the baskets, and carried the chickens inside to keep them safe for the night. Each morning at daybreak, the children got up and let the chickens out. Then the chickens did what most people in Liberia do every day—scratched the land for something to eat.

There isn't much mystery surrounding chickens. They function on instinct. Generation after generation, they are the same. They scratch for food. The rooster mates with the hens. The hens lay eggs and sit on them. The eggs hatch. Chicks become a shadow of the hen and learn how to keep from being eaten by the hawk. They roost and start the day over again. Some eventually become dinner. It's a constant cycle.

As I sat with Mr. Wiah, I became philosophical myself. *Some people are as predictable as these chickens*, I thought. *They go about life every day living the same worn-out, predictable patterns of life. They have no desire to change—no desire to learn, to make a new friend, read a new book, travel anywhere new, try different foods, or listen to a new genre of music. They live with the same prejudices as their parents and discriminate against the same kinds of people. They are as predictable as the rising and the setting of the sun.*

All of us need a certain amount of familiarity to make life manageable and recognizable. We all need to find our way back to a familiar and comfortable home every night where we can rest with the assurance of safety. We need familiar faces and caring people surrounding us in order to know we are loved. We need familiar words of Scripture to comfort us when we feel distraught and discouraged.

We need the familiar because, whether we like change or not, change happens. When our world

A young girl pulls a bucket of water from a well near her home. Children learn at an early age to help with the chores of daily life.

suddenly changes around us, we need to hold on to something familiar to calm our anxieties. Our most important assurance is knowing that God is still with us, that God has not abandoned us, and that God still loves us.

Even though every Liberian is a person of color, Liberia has been a divided country since freed slaves founded it in 1847. From the landing of the *Elizabeth,* the freed slaves struggled with the indigenous people of the country. For more than a century, the Americo-Liberians tried to stifle change. They tried to retain power, and they tried to keep the landscape around them as familiar as possible.

Change was inevitable. Instead of Liberia finding a leader who would spread wings over all the people, both those native to Africa and those with American slave ancestry, the leaders pecked out the indigenous people from roles of power or promise. Finally, the indigenous people rebelled against the pecking order of the Americo-Liberians. When they rose up, Liberia imploded.

Notes

1. "Population and the Environment," Day of 6 Billion Information Kit, http://www.unfpa.org/6billion/ccmc/environment.html, September 1999.

2. Charles Kuralt, *A Life on the Road* (New York: Ivy Books, 1990) 186.

3. These groups include Alden Baptist Church, Springfield, Massachusetts; Baptist World Alliance; Brookstone School, Columbus, Georgia; Cape Fear Otolaryngology of Fayetteville, North Carolina; Counterpart International, Washington, D.C.; Ebenezer Baptist Church, Charlotte, North Carolina; Ebenezer Baptist Church, Providence, Rhode Island; Family Dentistry of Hope Mills, North Carolina; Fellowship Baptist Church of Allen, Texas; First Baptist Church of Christ, Macon, Georgia; First Baptist Church, Columbus, Georgia; First Baptist Church, El Dorado, Kansas; First Baptist Church, Frankfort, Kentucky; First Baptist Church, Jonesboro, Georgia; First Baptist Church, Rome, Georgia; First Baptist Church, San Angelo, Texas; Green Acres Baptist Church, Tyler, Texas; International Ministries-American Baptist Churches, Valley Forge, Pennsylvania; Lambert Memorial Baptist Church, North Carolina; Lewis Chapel Missionary Baptist Church, Fayetteville, North Carolina; Lovejoy Baptist Church, Lovejoy, Georgia; Maranacook School, Maine; Metropolitan Baptist Church, Dorchester, Massachusetts; Milledge Avenue Baptist Church, Athens, Georgia; Morningstar Treatment Services, Inc., Georgia; Mt. Pisgah Missionary Baptist Church, Raeford, North Carolina; Oak Hill Academy, Mouth of Wilson, Virginia; Passport Camps, Inc.; Restoration Missionary Baptist Church of Fayetteville, North Carolina; Ricks Institute Alumni Association, Inc.; Sonoraville Baptist Church, Calhoun, Georgia; the Cooperative Baptist Fellowship; the Cooperative Baptist Fellowship of Georgia; the U.S. Embassy; Trinity Baptist Church, Moultrie, Georgia; Union Baptist Association of Fayetteville, North Carolina; Union Baptist Association, North Carolina; Woman's Missionary Union in Birmingham, Alabama; World Vision; and World Wide Word.

Chapter 13

Two More Starfish in the Sea

Henry Peabody's parents couldn't attend his college graduation. They remained in Liberia, struggling like all other Liberians to survive. Even so, on Mother's Day 2002, I knew Mr. and Mrs. Peabody's thoughts were with their son, who was receiving his college degree, a Bachelor of Science with a major in sociology and a minor in Christianity, from Mercer University.

I first met Henry in December 1995 at a worship service in the chapel of the Liberian Baptist Theological Seminary in Paynesville, Liberia, just outside of Monrovia. At the time, seminary students attended school at a temporary location in Monrovia because the ECOMOG peacekeeping troops used the seminary as a base. However, on that day, many of the students came to the chapel on the school's campus for the special service. We sang hymns. Then people stood and gave testimonies of praise to God for the chance to go to school and for sparing their lives during the war. In spite of the hardships of war, in spite of the losses they had suffered, these students were filled with joy and hope.

Although Henry Peabody was not a seminary student, he rose to give praise to God. Henry had recently returned from a refugee camp in Ghana. Henry, like thousands of other Liberians, left the country when the bullets began flying, seeking refuge. He grew up in the Firestone area where his father worked. Firestone has one million acres of rubber trees, but the fourteen-year civil war shut down production as it did all other industry. Today, after more than eighty years of investment, Firestone still has the largest rubber operation in the world in Liberia, covering almost 200 square miles.

Henry moved into Monrovia when he was in the tenth grade. Like Olu Menjay, when the war began, Henry had completed his high school work but never had the opportunity to graduate. When the fighting came to the city, Henry was unable to make it back home. He found refuge with a friend in another part of the city. He stayed there for one month before they ran out of food. Henry and his friend went into Monrovia to the market in search of food. While there, they were arrested by a member of the Armed Forces of Liberia (AFL), rebels loyal to former president Samuel Doe. One of the groups opposing the AFL often wore red hats and red T-shirts. Henry was wearing a red T-shirt, and it almost cost him his life. After the arrest, he and his friend were told they would be executed. As they waited on a vehicle to transport them to the beach for execution, one of Doe's soldiers drove by, identified Henry and his friend, and ordered them freed.

Once they returned home, they decided they needed to leave the area, lest someone mistake them again for rebels. The next time, they might not be as fortunate. They crossed the bridge into the New Kru Town area. They didn't know anyone there, so they slept outside for several days. Finally, a family gave them refuge, but there was no food. Many days, Henry survived only on water.

Word came that a ship was leaving for Ghana to take people who wanted to escape the fighting. Henry decided to join them. "I was not sure where I was going. I did not know what I was doing. I had no money. I had nothing," Henry recalled in a conversation with me. The ship represented hope and survival. Those left behind faced a rising sea of struggle and death. As the ship left the Monrovian harbor, it marked the first time Henry had traveled outside the borders of his country. In fact, he'd never traveled far from the Firestone and Monrovia areas. Now he was forced to find refuge in a foreign land.

Before boarding the ship, he found a jar of mayonnaise in a looted box taken from a warehouse at the port. He survived on that jar of mayonnaise for two days aboard the ship before it left Monrovia and for the three days it took the ship to arrive in Ghana.

Henry became sick and lost consciousness en route to Ghana. He awoke to people speaking French in a hospital in Accra, Ghana. After regaining strength, he was transported to the Buduburam Refugee Camp, located twenty-seven miles west of the city. The camp was home to more than 35,000 Liberian refugees during the Liberian civil war. While the refugee camp provided safety from the Liberian rebels, existence in the Buduburam camp was not much more than a life of survival. Refugee families, who endured long stretches of boredom, were typically given a small structure the size of one or two western bedrooms. However, with temperatures sweltering higher than 100 degrees, few people stayed inside during the day. They slept in their rooms because they had no other choice, and they stored their few possessions there.

While in Ghana, the refugees were not allowed to work outside the camp. Some ran small stalls; some traded with others in the camp. A few people made clothes and others made furniture. The refugees spent most of the time outside their homes cooking, washing, sitting, and talking. Day after day, week after week, month after month, year after year, the refugees waited for news that the war would soon end and they could return home. When Henry arrived, he had little idea that the camp would be his home for the next five years.

Henry formed many friendships during his years in the refugee camp. Perhaps none were more important than his friendship with Hugo Menjay, brother of Olu. Henry had never met Hugo before they encountered one another at the refugee camp, but he knew Hugo's brother Olu from his early childhood, when he was involved in the Royal Ambassador program of his church. During the summers, Henry and Olu saw each other at Royal Ambassador camp. Henry had already been in the refugee camp for more than a year when Hugo arrived. Henry and Hugo spent a lot of time together, even sharing a room at the camp.

After five years of exile in Ghana, Henry decided it was safe to return to Liberia, which had regained some stability. There was a fragile peace. He returned by bus to a country with no electricity or running water. The war had destroyed most of the country's infrastructure. Schools were nonexistent. Nevertheless, the churches were full, and he found that for most Christians, their faith, though tested, had sustained them. God was still present among them despite the war.

Henry had not been back in Liberia for long when I met him that December day at the seminary. I remember him standing in the prayer service and praising God for bringing him through the war, through the years as a refugee, and back home again after such a long time away. He talked about God's faithfulness and of how God saw him through trial after trial.

After the service, I talked briefly with Henry. He asked for my address. I bade him farewell, never imagining that we'd meet again or what God had in store for either of us. That was December 1995. In April 1996, the city of Monrovia fell to rebels. The peacekeeping shield provided by ECOMOG failed. The rebels made their run on the city, and a new wave of violence and savage killing was unleashed on the helpless people of Monrovia.

Henry again faced the decision of whether he should stay in the country or flee. He found two of Charles Taylor's soldiers who were traveling by car to the Ivory Coast border. Although it was a risky decision, he asked for a ride. Sitting between rebel soldiers with machine guns was far from comforting. Henry knew that at any moment these men could be involved in a gun battle with enemy forces. However, the risk paid off. He made it to the Ivory Coast border. Once across the border, he found people he knew who helped him make his way back to the refugee camp in Ghana.

From the day we met at the seminary until the day Henry arrived back in Ghana, more than four months had passed. Although Henry had little more than the clothes on his back, he had kept my address. On May 16, 1996, I received the following letter from Henry with the return address marked "Buduburam Refugee Camp, National Mobilization."

> Dear Dr. Helms, Grace, peace and mercy be unto you in the name of our Lord and Savior Jesus Christ. Indeed the Lord is good. Let's continue to praise Him. Exactly five months ago you were in Liberia teaching and encouraging us to have hope, hope in changing times. This was a great message. I was greatly impressed by your love and concern for us. On Friday, April 5, after attending the Good Friday service, I decided to visit a friend on my way home. I was told that a new war had started and I could not go home. I decided to wait for Saturday, April 6. Upon waking up, I could see everyone moving from one end to another. Then I said to myself, "Yes, it's really a new war!" I could not go home again. After two weeks I made an attempt to go home. When I got to my house all my things were gone. My entire house was stripped of everything. But thanks be to God, I still have life. I had just returned home after five years of refugee life in Ghana, when I sit and wonder what kind of hardship we are going through. I still remember God's message through you. There's still hope. Dr. Helms, I'm in a very desperate need of some emergency assistance and would be very grateful if you will come to my aid at this time. I'm in need of some clothing. My trouser size is 34/36; shirt or t-shirt size is large; shoe size or sneaker size is 10½; brief, medium; socks, towels, soap, deodorant. I will be very grateful Dr. Helms if you will come to my aid at once. I'm in a desperate condition since I returned from Liberia. You can send these things by mail. I will get it. If you cannot send these things now, even a check will help. I look forward to your timely response. Love in Jesus, Brother Henry Peabody.

Members of my church in Clarkesville helped me gather the things Henry asked for and more, not knowing whether he would receive them. After all, how reliable is an address in a refugee camp? The package cost more to send than the items in the package were worth, but we knew that if Henry got them, they would be a huge encouragement to him.

Henry received the package, which prompted another letter. Henry wrote, "I'm encouraged Dr. Helms that our God is a living God. One day I know these hardships will be over. I know His promise is true. The crime rate is high here. Everybody's doing something to survive. We have terrible criminals here. If you leave your house in the morning to go out, if you are not careful you will lose all your things. Living here on a day-to-day basis is like singing a song that has no end."

One person missing from the camp when Henry returned was Hugo Menjay. Henry learned that Olu was able to arrange for Hugo to travel to the States to study at Truett-McConnell College. Hugo had left for Liberia to get a visa and was off to America. Hugo's good fortune gave Henry hope. It actually changed his entire thinking process. "If it can happen to Hugo, why can't it happen for me?" Henry wondered. This optimism became evident in Henry's letters. He began to ask me if I would help him come to the States to study. "My only hope," he'd write, "is to be able to get an education."

My immediate reaction was the same as when Caleb Dormah asked me to travel to Liberia to speak at YouthChallenge Liberia in 1995: "That's too much to ask. There's no way!" The commitment to educate someone in college is astronomical. "Besides," I thought, "in a few years, I'll have my own children to educate." How could I possibly make such a commitment? Was bringing a Liberian to the States even the right thing to do? Where would all the money come from? Could I even get a college to accept him?

I tried to dismiss the idea, but I never got it out of my mind. I kept thinking of the biblical story of the "beggar named Lazarus, covered with sores, longing to eat what fell from the rich man's table. Even the dogs came and licked his sores" (Luke 16:20b-21, NIV). I knew I was the rich man. I knew Henry was Lazarus. "There will always be rich men and there will always be a Lazarus who needs help," I rationalized. Furthermore, "What good would helping just one do in a sea of so many?"

I tried to dismiss the thought. It was too expensive. It was risky. It was foolish. Wouldn't people laugh at me? I cannot share all the details because they are too personal, but the Lord finally convinced me that he would take care of my children's needs if I'd be faithful and take care of Henry. God convinced me that he would surround me with help to supply Henry's needs if I took a step in faith. As soon as I became obedient and started the process, God began opening doors.

First, I had to get Henry accepted to a college. That's not easy when a person has no high school diploma, no ACT or SAT scores. Try convincing people at a college that you know a man living in a refugee camp in Ghana who wants to attend. He'll come if they will let him enroll in school without jumping through all the hoops. They look at you strangely.

I didn't have an inroad to a college president or a trustee. I had to go through the normal channels, so I got knocked around like a ping-pong ball until people began to understand that in order for Henry to be admitted to college, they would have to waive many of the normal procedures. When I finally got people to understand and accept that, we made progress.

Once Henry was accepted for classes for the fall semester at Truett-McConnell College, I had to work with the United States Embassy to issue him a visa, which was even more difficult. In order to get Henry to the United States, I had to get him back to Liberia, where he would have to wait for a visa. We didn't know how long it would take. Finally, I had to raise money to get him to the States. A plane ticket to America cost about $2,000. We would be down $2,000 before the first semester's school bill ever became due. I am not good at asking people for money. I prayed about this matter, and money came from people unsolicited when they learned of the need. It was amazing to watch God work.

Here's one of the great ironies of this story: Who do you think was waiting to become Henry's roommate at Truett-McConnell College in 1997? Hugo Menjay. These two young men went from rooming together at the Buduburam Refugee Camp to rooming together at a Baptist college in North Georgia. Only God could accomplish such a miracle.

With scholarship money for playing on the soccer team and other financial aid, we were able to get Henry's tuition down to a manageable level, but there were constant bills. Praise God, we always had money to meet his expenses! God always provided.

After two years of study at Truett-McConnell College, Henry transferred to Mercer University. As Olu said to Dr. Hinson, there were cheaper choices, but not better ones. Although we did get scholarship help at Mercer, our bills increased sharply. I didn't have the same pull at Truett-McConnell as Dr. Carpenter did with Olu, or the same pull at Mercer as Dr. Hinson did. However, this only served to increase my faith that God was faithful to supply our needs. We never missed a payment for Henry's college expenses. Without the help of numerous people, my wife and I would not have been able to keep up with the college tuition. We were humbled that God directed people, mostly without our asking, to contribute to Henry's expenses every semester.

Henry amazed us with his ability to maintain good grades and with his desire to serve the Lord. In summer 2000, he served as a missionary to South Korea. He spent most of his time teaching the South Koreans how to play soccer. He used that as an opportunity to share his personal story. The South Koreans were eager to learn how to play soccer and they were intrigued with Henry. They all wanted to know how a Liberian ended up in South Korea via America. God gave Henry a unique platform that he used to his advantage for sharing the gospel. That summer, Henry led several South Koreans to the Lord. Today, lives in South Korea are changed because God led us to rescue a Liberian from a Ghanaian refugee camp, bring him to the United States, and then support him as he decided to serve as a missionary to South Korea.

Henry received his diploma from Mercer's then-president Kirby Godsey in 2002. As I witnessed Henry's graduation, I thanked God for those who helped us save one individual from a hopeless life. With many others helping us, we were able to put one more starfish filled with hope and promise into the sea of life. Praise the Lord!

Today Henry is married to a native Liberian, and he works in inner-city Philadelphia as a social worker. He pastors a small Liberian community of believers.

There are many Liberians like Henry living in the United States. Prior to the Liberian civil war, the primary reasons Liberians entered the United States were business, pleasure, and student and exchange visitation, with a majority returning to Liberia. After the war began, the immigration status of Liberians entering the United States started to change. Liberians began to receive new immigration classifications that allowed them to remain in the country. Some were issued immigrant visas (given to those desiring permanent residency status with the issue of a green card), asylum (those already in the United States who did not want to return to their country because they feared persecution due to race, religion, nationality, or membership in a particular social or political group), and refugee status (those outside their country who were unable or unwilling to return because of persecution on account of race, religion, nationality, or membership in a particular social or political group).

The numbers of Liberians entering the United States rose dramatically as well. Between 1980 and 2003, the number totaled 110,589. About half that number received permanent status. The United States has opened her arms to many like these from dozens of nations: battered, bruised, hungry, willing to work, hoping for a future and opportunity. Yet there is a limit to the number we can allow.

Our decision to be responsible for bringing a refugee to the United States wasn't made easily. Plenty of people native to America get washed up on the shores of life and need our financial help as well. Our resources are limited. Yet we cannot be so narrow in our focus that we help only those within our country.

I have struggled with another issue. In many third-world countries, brain drain is a common problem. Those with the most potential, those with some financial means, and those best educated are usually the first to find their way out of the deteriorating conditions of a third-world country in times of crisis, often never to return to assist their people. Once these people make it to America and become accustomed to the American way of life, returning to a country where the literacy rate is only 20 percent and the unemployment rate is 85 percent is considered too great a sacrifice. Indeed, it may even be economic suicide. It makes more sense for those who come to America for asylum to stay in this country, earn a living, and send money back to their families in Liberia.

Many immigrants come into America with the promise of returning home once they complete their education or once it is safe. Promises such as these tend to vaporize. This is the land of opportunity. America and her comforts, opportunities, and amenities are not easy to give up once they become part of a person's daily life. It's not difficult to understand why those who come as refugees want to stay should our government allow it. What if they return home and the circumstances deteriorate again? Next time, they might not be as fortunate to escape.

Had we not brought Henry to America, he would struggle to eat today. Instead, he is working toward a master's degree and helping dysfunctional families in America, as well as helping his aging parents in Liberia buy food. He may yet return to Liberia to teach or work in another area once he is awarded permanent status in America, which will give him the freedom to come and go without fear of getting stuck in Liberia should fighting break out again. As long as Liberia offers no jobs, there is little incentive for people like Henry to return.

Perhaps a better way to help the Liberian people is the way I agreed to help Dorris Seh. Dorris graduated from Ricks Institute at age twenty. Like most of her generation, she found that the Liberian civil war interrupted her studies more than once. To her credit, she was determined to complete her high school studies. In 2003, that part of her life's dream came true.

I met Dorris in 2006 on my second trip to Liberia. Dr. Olu Menjay introduced her to me on the campus of Ricks Institute. Dr. Menjay told me that during the 2003 presidential campaign, presidential candidate George Weah came to the school to speak to the students. Weah was a former international soccer star, having played with the prestigious Italian A. C. Milan, with whom he won the Golden Ball award for being the best European player and also the Italian National Championship in 1995. In that year, Weah was also named the World Player of the Year. This made him a national hero in Liberia.

Dorris Seh, a nursing graduate from Cuttington University, and her father, Varney Seh, head of security at Ricks Institute, both survived the rebels' attack on the Ricks campus in 1996.

After his speech at Ricks Institute, Weah awarded a college scholarship, as he was doing throughout the country. Awarding scholarships was tantamount to buying votes, but it wasn't illegal, and it endeared him to the people. Dorris Seh received one of his scholarships. Receiving that award meant her dream of becoming a nurse could come true. Following graduation from Ricks Institute, she enrolled in nursing school at Cuttington University. After Weah lost the election to Ellen Johnson-Sirleaf, however, his benevolent spirit vanished. All scholarships were revoked, dashing the dreams of people like Dorris.

Like most Liberian children, Dorris had endured a difficult life. She was five years old when the war began. Her family lived on the east side of Monrovia. When the rebels came to the city, Dorris was much older. As the oldest in the family, she helped her mother care for seven brothers and sisters.

When the rebels arrived, the family had to flee and live in the bush. Her father, Varney, often left his family to search for food. Sometimes he was gone for a day or two. When he came back, he might bring only a little cassava. During one point, the family spent an entire month in the bush trying to avoid rebel soldiers, but they were not always successful. Some nights the rebels came and took everything that belonged to the family. Once, the rebels threatened to kill Varney, but after he begged for his life, they let him go.

Eventually, the family settled in the Virginia area near Ricks Institute where Dorris and her siblings attended. As time elapsed, the war found them even there. In 1996, rebels attacked the campus. Dorris was in the ninth grade at the time, and she remembers hearing gunfire in the distance. At first, the school administrators downplayed the sounds, but the gunfire grew closer and louder. Finally, the administrators decided to hurry and get the students off campus.

At the time, Ricks Institute owned a bus. Varney was responsible for driving children to and from school. Varney said to me, "When we heard the first rocket attack, we put the children in the bus and took them as far as Brewerville. We turned around to come get the second group off campus; it was terrible. We saw a large crowd running. We stopped at the main gate. We had to hold the students' hands as everyone was fighting to get off campus. My children ran to our home [just down the road from the school] with my oldest daughter Dorris."

He continued, "We got to the creek on the road and the bus could not go because there were so many people hanging on it by the road. The rebels had already overpowered the government troops and captured the campus. I managed to make my way through the bush to my house, where I found my children. We left my home and went to a displacement camp. The rebels looted the campus and killed all the animals."

The family went to the displacement camp at Graystone near the U.S. Embassy. At this point, Varney became separated from his family by the river and did not see them again for six months. When they were finally reunited, Varney discovered his family had no food, so he left them again in search of something to feed his family. "Finding food was really difficult," Varney said. "People who had food didn't want to let go of it because people wanted to keep what they had for their own family. If you found food and returned to your family by the road, it was greatly reduced by the rebels by the time you arrived." Varney said that not being able to find food for his family was the worst experience of his life. "In Liberia, if you don't bring home a bag of beggar's rice in a month, your family downplays you," he said. Even though he did not feel responsible for the war, he felt responsible for not being able to find food. He maintained hope that his children would not be disgraced (raped) as so many had. He maintained hope that the war would end and the school would reopen.

At the war's end, Dr. Menjay became God's fulfillment of hope for Varney Seh. Dr. Menjay arrived on the campus in 2005 to reopen Ricks Institute. Varney was one of the first men to work for Dr. Menjay. "Mr. Seh," as Dr. Menjay respectfully calls him, is the head of security at the school. He is trustworthy and has proven himself a valuable asset to Dr. Menjay and the staff.

When I visited the school in 2006, Dr. Menjay introduced me to Mr. Seh and then to his daughter Dorris. He told me Dorris's story and of her deep desire to continue her studies in nursing school. Dr. Menjay said to me, "If you decide to help anyone because of your visit to us, I'd like you to help this young woman. She's very deserving and she will make a good nurse. We could use a good nurse here at Ricks Institute."

Late one evening, I walked from the school to visit the Seh family. I knew Varney supported his entire family on a few hundred dollars a year. One year's tuition at Cuttington University is about six times what he makes in a year. Dorris had completed one year at the school and had no hope of returning without help. With no education, Dorris would become like most young women in Liberia—she would be forced into an early marriage and to depend upon a male to provide an income for her. Children would come soon thereafter, followed by the hard cycle of life. Life from that point would consist of poverty with many mouths to feed and long hours of difficult physical labor.

Before then-president George Weah came to the school, Dorris had prayed for a scholarship. She had prayed and fasted for a week for God to send her help so she could continue her schooling. After her hopes were dashed, she had prayed again for God to find a way for her to attend school. A career in nursing meant hope not just for Dorris, but for others. She wanted to help other people in need. "With God's help after achieving my education, it is my goal to help those who are dying. My whole goal is to help others, to help save lives and to share with others," Dorris told me.

That evening as darkness fell, I sat with the Seh family and promised to make it financially possible for Dorris to complete her college degree, provided she would become a nurse at Ricks Institute for one year following her graduation. It would be a paid position. Following that year, she could look for another job or continue working as a nurse at the school. By the world's standards, Dorris will always be poor. By Liberia's standards, she is going to have a chance to escape the worst of the poverty. Most importantly, she is going to escape the hopelessness so many Liberians feel because they have no education and no ability to produce income.

I don't think I've ever extended a gift to anyone who was as grateful as this family. Through tears of joy, the Seh family expressed their gratitude. The younger children looked on with odd curiosity at the white man sitting with their family in the dusk of the day, offering a college education to their older sister. The words of Jesus were never more real: "It is more blessed to give than to receive" (Acts 20:35, KJV).

In April 2008, I received this email from Dorris:

> Dear Pastor and Brethren in Christ, I greet you all in the name of our Lord and Savior Jesus Christ. I hope you all are doing well. Our nursing college will be honoring all nurses on May 3, 2008. I have been selected as one of those nurses to be honored. This program is a traditional program for all nurses, which includes capping of nurses. In this light I am kindly informing you all that I am going to be capped, and also honored as a practical nurse. I am so grateful to God and my appreciation goes to you all for your numerous contributions toward my studies. May God richly bless you all and continue to provide for you all.
>
> Dorris Seh, Nursing Student, Cuttington University

I made my promise to her in good faith that others would join me in helping pay for Dorris's tuition. In 2009, members of Trinity Baptist helped complete the last payment on her nursing fees. Also, the church of my youth, the church that ordained me, Louisville Baptist Church in Louisville, Alabama, was gracious in adopting Dorris and helping with her tuition. Others have also helped along the way. Dorris graduated in May 2009.

Dorris will be able to play an important role in the healing process of Liberia. She will help save many lives in a land of few doctors. She will assist the dying. Along with her skills, she has the compassion needed to minister to the entire person. She will treat the young and the old, the hungry and the tired, the frightened and the lonely. Dorris Seh will unashamedly give witness to her Lord as she binds up wounds and cares for the sick.

We can't save every Liberian, but we have managed to save Henry and Dorris.[1] We put two more starfish into the sea of educated, productive citizens of the world. One is making a difference to troubled Americans in inner-city Philadelphia and also pastoring a Liberian congregation. The other is making a difference in her native land of Liberia, healing the sick, tending to the dying, and bringing hope to the tired and weary who need the compassion and love of a Christian nurse.

Note

1. God kept his promise to me that if I took care of Henry's education, he would take care of my children. While we saved money faithfully for our children's college education through the years, my older son currently serves as a lance corporal in the U.S. Marine Corps. The recently improved G.I. Bill will give John nearly $50,000 to use for college once he completes his military experience. Our younger son, Ryan, is a U.S.A. Diving National Champion and is attending the University of Tennessee on a diving scholarship. God has taken care of our college needs. God is faithful!

Chapter 14

Hoping the Least of These with the Essentials of Life

Visible from the front steps of the guest residence at Ricks Institute is the concrete outline of a grave. A closer look reveals the name on the grave: Southern Baptist Missionary, Virginia Lee Land Mills. The date of her death is marked June 23, 1971. Virginia's grave is juxtaposed with an unmarked grave of a rebel soldier, a stark reminder that the Ricks Institute's campus lost its innocence when it became the front lines in the latter stages of the Liberian civil war.

One morning I stood at Virginia's grave pondering what may have happened to her, and a teacher from Ricks called out to me as he walked down the dirt road toward the school. "Mrs. Ginny was my teacher," he said. "She taught literature. She was a very good teacher." Still walking, he said, "She got sick and died after being here only two years. Her husband taught biology." Ginny represents hundreds of men and women, Liberian and foreign born, who have given a small or large part of their lives to educate the children and youth of Ricks Institute since the school's founding in 1887.

A glance at course requirements during the school's early years shows the educational emphasis at that time. A course in Bible was a yearly requirement in the primary division. Other subjects included spelling, reading, geography, penmanship, and mental arithmetic. The intermediate division studied the Bible along with reading, penmanship, English grammar, geography, higher arithmetic, algebra, Latin, Arabic, Vey, Mandingo, history of Liberia, general history, English composition and declamation, and vocal music. The inclusion of Vey, Mandingo, and Arabic was an obvious sign and a strong statement to the indigenous population that their culture mattered. If those in government positions had taken a similar approach, Liberia's relationship with the indigenous population would have been better and her future might have turned out differently.

In addition to these subjects, in the earlier stages of the school, students maintained about forty acres of planted crops. The students were required to help raise their own food, growing crops such as coffee, eddoes, plantain, and cassava and selling the surplus in the market to generate money for the school. An old adage was applied in Liberia at that time: "Give a man a fish and you've fed him for a day. Teach him to fish and you've fed him for a life-time." These students did not just eat the food grown from the Ricks acreage; they also learned how to grow food for themselves.

Helping students learn to care for themselves was a high priority for the school from its inception. Moses Ricks believed education and missions were vital for the success of Liberia, and the only way for these objectives to remain profitable in Liberia was for the people to take care of their own needs. For decades, Ricks students raised pigs, chickens, eggs, and vegetable crops, which generated resources for the school's operation. Mr. Isaac Davis, a former student and employee for more than twenty-seven years at Ricks, recalls that Ricks Institute generated a substantial amount of income from selling chickens, pigs, and vegetables to retailers in the Monrovia market. Rabbits, which are high in protein, were fed to the students in the campus dining hall and sold in the market. Mr. Davis recalls that most of the foods served to students in the dining halls were grown or raised on the Ricks campus.

The financial help the school accepted came from within the Baptist family. Moses Ricks was a Baptist, and the school became affiliated with the Liberian Baptist Missionary and Education Convention. Fundraising events by the Woman's Missionary Union (WMU) and the trustees of the school were deemed appropriate and did not take away from the school's original mission of being self-sustaining. Missionary Edward Blyden rightly noted that when a woman "understands and cooperates with any work, it will move on." The work of the WMU was vital throughout the school's history.

Since the 1960s, Ricks Institute had received money from the Southern Baptist Convention. The school had become a point of entry into the coun-try for Southern Baptists. Money was used to construct administrative buildings and dormitories. The cafeteria was named after H. Cornell Gorner, Area Secretary for West Africa for the Foreign Mission Board. In the 1970s, the government of Liberia offered Ricks Institute money as a token of appre-ciation for its work in providing an important educational service for its citizens. As mentioned earlier, this government money posed a conflict of interest for Southern Baptists, long supporters of the separation of church and state. However, changes in the distribution of funds to Ricks Institute were not made until Rev. Cornell Gorner's retirement. Then, in the late 1970s, Ricks Institute lost $75,000 in support from Southern Baptists.[1] However, missionary personnel were not withdrawn from the campus. Missionary presence remained on the campus until the war drove them out in May/June 1990.

After Southern Baptists withdrew financial support, Ricks became dependent on government money. Other supporters developed a welfare mentality and stopped contributing as well. When the government funds dried up, Ricks was left without a base of support. The school had gotten away from its original charter of being a self-sustaining school, and then it paid a huge price. Of course, the war would have dried up the funds anyway, but the school was hurting financially even before the war. By that time, a dependent mindset was in place at Ricks.

Dr. Menjay has the desire to carry Ricks back to her original charter of being self-sustaining. Presently, his goal is out of reach. The school depends on outside help for a large percentage of its operating budget. Little by little, Liberians must learn the philosophy of Moses Ricks: that education and missions are vital for every Liberian, and the only way for these objectives to remain profitable in Liberia is by Liberians doing these tasks for themselves.

This will take time. The war frustrated efforts to grow and harvest crops. No one could stay in one place long enough to plant and harvest. When fruits and vegetables came in season, the rebels took them for themselves. It's been almost a generation since children were taught how to plant and harvest. They must relearn these skills.

Dr. Menjay didn't realize the extent of the children's hunger when he first began as principal. In his first year, some Americans visited the school and started giving out candy. Every child loves candy, but the scene resembled a shopaholic's mad dash into stores on America's day after Thanksgiving sale. Some of the children began fighting one another for the candy, afraid they would be left out. Dr. Menjay realized these children weren't fighting to feed their sugar habit. These children were fighting to feed their hunger. He asked himself, "How can children learn when they are preoccupied with hunger? How can a teacher hold their attention when the children are hungry?"

Even though the Liberian civil war is over, Dr. Menjay has many battles left to fight in this war-stricken land. Hunger is one of those battles. He realized it was irrational to offer children knowledge while they battled the pains

Children lick the bowl after a meal is being prepared for the Ricks students.

of hunger. He made the commitment that the school would begin a feeding program as a part of its mission. The school began feeding the children on Tuesdays, Wednesdays, and Thursdays of each week. Now the program has been expanded to five days a week. The children arrive at school knowing they will receive a cooked meal of rice, topped off with potato greens or fish-head soup. The meals are provided to the children without charge. Partnering churches and organizations, mostly from America, make these meals possible.

Everyone at the school is fed, including teachers and workers. The feeding program has produced visible results. The children who stand in the lunch line at Ricks are happy to receive a warm meal. Smiles and laughter fill the eating area. The workers exhibit an increased morale. The food has given the children hope that things are getting better in Liberia.

The Cooperative Baptist Fellowship of Georgia donated money that helped supply a fresh coat of paint in the cafeteria. Paintings by Patrick Lokoua, the French teacher at the school, adorn the walls, giving the cafeteria a warm Liberian feeling. People made new tabletops to replace those destroyed during the war. There is hope that the war on hunger can be won in time.

When Ricks began serving food, school attendance increased. Children even come to school sick because they know they will get to eat. James

Flomo, a ninth grader, writes, "Hunger is like a house without a roof. As the result of this, fathers will not be respected by their wives or their children. In addition, children will leave the home for the street in order to find food for themselves."

Since the inception of the feeding program, teachers have noticed an increase in test scores. Although it's difficult to measure, a child who is not hungry is a happier child; a happier child will attend school more often; a child who attends school more often receives a better education. When the feeding program began, $25 (U.S.) purchased a 100-pound bag of rice. The world's economy affects third-world countries as well. Now the price for a 100-pound bag of rice is $38. The commitment to feed the children three meals per week is $230.

Dr. Menjay is not merely looking for handouts. His long-term goal is to overcome the food shortage by using the vast acreage available to the school to grow food and raise animals. Although rice is the staple food of Liberia and must be imported, the grounds of the campus are fertile. Currently, watermelons, cassava, peppers, and sweet potatoes are grown. The school now requires all students, seventh through twelfth grades, to take agriculture as a subject. Twenty percent of the subject is theory, and eighty percent is practical. These children learn to feed themselves, and, given the proper vision, they also learn to provide for their families through growing and selling crops.

In addition to food, the need for safe drinking water abounds in Liberia. In America, we rarely think about this basic need. Every faucet we turn on offers safe water. Only when we are struck with a natural disaster do we become concerned about our own drinking supply. In Liberia, no faucets operated for more than fourteen years. The first ones began working again in 2007. Most water is still drawn from wells, but wells in Liberia are shallow. Since the water is close to the surface and the temperature stays warm year-round, bacteria grows in the well water, contributing to a large number of waterborne diseases. In developing countries like Liberia, four-fifths of all illnesses are caused by waterborne diseases, with diarrhea being the leading cause of childhood death.

The civil war affected everyone. Even the capitol was without the basic use of a flushable toilet. I was shocked to discover this when we visited in 2006. Vice President Joseph Boakai is also a trustee of the Liberian Baptist Theological Seminary and a deacon of Effort Baptist Church. Since I had served as a member of a steering committee responsible for moving funds to the seminary, we had issues to discuss. Earlier in the week, Boakai had invited Dr. Menjay and me to his home to discuss those issues. Our visit led to his invitation to the dedication of his newly renovated office space. From his office, I could see the beauty of the Atlantic Ocean. Even though his office was beautifully adorned with newly laid carpet and comfortable chairs, there wasn't a functional bathroom in the entire building.

I was honored to voice a prayer of dedication for his new office. After the prayer, we talked about the future of Liberia. As we talked, other Liberians were busy working to make life more comfortable for the people in the capitol. Directly

Twin girls taken to the river by their mother to wash their clothes and give them a bath.

behind the capitol is one of the few functioning wells in the city. Strong men drew water from the well and carried the containers up several flights of stairs to supply water to the bathrooms and to members of Congress. A gallon of water weighs 8.33 lbs. Five gallons weigh 41.65 pounds. I watched as young men carried two five-gallon containers at a time up several flights of stairs. This was their job all day.

Like the city of Jerusalem, the city of Monrovia sits on a hill. But unlike the city of Jerusalem, which received water through an underground tunnel built in the days of King Hezekiah, Monrovia suffered throughout the fourteen-year civil war and years thereafter without a functional water and sewer system.

Because of its location on a hill, getting water uphill was no easy task. During my time in Monrovia, I watched as strong teenage boys began their day at various distribution points just outside the city, where massive tanks of fresh water stand. There the boys filled about twenty five-gallon jerry cans with water, which they placed on a rolling cart. Then they began the arduous task of pulling and pushing this cart uphill, filled with about 800 pounds of water. They crossed a bridge and pushed the cart uphill and into the city, covering about a mile. Once in the city, they sold the five-gallon cans of water for five Liberian dollars, about ten American cents. They did this all day, making about two American dollars in wages.

Water issues existed on the campus of Ricks Institute as well. The school had a water tower that was built decades ago. Gunfire during the war riddled the tank with holes, but it was repaired and able to hold water. A previous mission team had run water lines to a couple of houses and all the way to the school. Some campus residents had their own wells, but most people had to walk long distances with their water cans and buckets. The inconvenience and hard work of carrying this water to their homes was enough for anyone to wish for tap water to flow again.

At Ricks Institute, children had used pit latrines as bathroom facilities for a dozen years. These latrines were disease factories. After visiting the school in 2006, I realized this was one of the school's most pressing needs. I came back home and began to work on a plan to get the water flowing on the campus of Ricks. Our church formed a relationship with the Cooperative Baptist Fellowship of Georgia, Milledge Ave. Baptist Church of Athens, Georgia, and the Moultrie Rotary Club. The $10,000 project helped us to purchase the PVC piping, toilets, sinks, and other supplies needed to get water flowing again into the school, cafeteria, and health clinic.

Money without skilled labor is nearly useless. I'm not a skilled plumber, woodworker, or electrician. I don't have those gifts. I do well just to unclog a toilet; never mind installing one. I prayed for God to send me those who could do the job. I presented the need to my congregation, and two men came forward—Farrell Tucker and Pat Tomlinson, both qualified plumbers. Both men served on the property committee at Trinity Baptist.

Once in Liberia, they used me for some of the smaller tasks and my sons, John and Ryan, for some of the muscle jobs. Mostly, they used the local Liberian men who worked at Ricks Institute to accomplish the task of replacing toilets and sinks in the boys' bathroom and getting water flowing into and out of the cafeteria and the health clinic. I was impressed with Farrell and Pat. After a couple of days, they realized that the local Liberians had skills. They realized that there was a Liberian way of doing things and an American way of doing things. In the end, what mattered wasn't which way was right or more efficient, but whether the job was accomplished.

I watched as these men backed away from projects enough to allow the Liberian men to do things their way, but not so far away that they allowed them to make a mistake that jeopardized the project. This gave the local men pride in their work, and in the process they also learned new skills and improved old ones.

When water came shooting out of an outdoor pipe for the first time in more than a decade and a half, we all acted like Texans who had hit a big oil gusher. Our work attracted the curiosity of the children. Most of these children had never used a flushable toilet or seen water flow into and out of a sink. Cries of joy came from the cooks the day the water started flowing in the cafeteria. No longer would these ladies have to take their kitchen pots, pans, and silverware outside to wash. Farrell wrote in his journal, "We got the water running in the cafeteria sinks—Olu says for the first time in seventeen years. Ruth, one of the school cooks, was so grateful, as was all the other kitchen staff. In concert with the inside water, we are installing a water-solar sanitation system."

The water-solar sanitation system Farrell noted in his journal was one of two he and Pat installed that was given to the school by the National Woman's Missionary Union. One was hooked up to the sink to rinse dishes. The other was hooked up to a water fountain in the cafeteria. All the children at Ricks now have access to purified drinking water.

Farrell's wife, Ellen, worked with the older girls at Ricks and taught them how to use a solar cooker to prepare meals. We prepared a couple of meals in the cooker to prove its worth. Liberians cook almost exclusively with charcoal, which is made from cutting down 4-to-6-inch diameter trees in the forest.[2] With three million people in Liberia using charcoal to cook their meals, it's easy to see that cutting the trees can become an issue. Solar cooking saves the forest and saves Liberians money, as the sun is a renewable resource.

Actions like these are vastly improving the health and self-sustaining abilities of those at Ricks. Most essential is that Liberians learn the skills and use the tools themselves. As more partnerships form with churches and groups to bring resources and ideas to the Liberian people, we envision a future in which the individuals at Ricks Institute and surrounding areas not only sustain themselves efficiently, but also teach others the same useful skills, improving life circumstances for many who would otherwise be without hope.

Notes

1. Incidentally, the loss in financial support for Ricks Institute became the gain of the Liberian Baptist Theological Seminary, which is where Southern Baptists shifted their funds. The added funds helped boost the seminary's status in the country and throughout the region of West Africa.

2. The stacked wood cut from the forest trees resembles a volcano with an opening at the top. The outside is packed with mud. A fire is started from the inside and the wood burns very slowly from the inside out. Once it's complete, the mud is removed leaving charcoal, which is then placed in large bags. A green leafy branch is placed over the opening of the bag and it's ready to be placed in a wheelbarrow or on the top of a vehicle to be transported to market.

Chapter 15

Jesus Is Still on the Move

As mentioned earlier, on our first trip to Liberia in 1995, Olu and I traveled to Ricks Institute. We met briefly with the principal and his wife. Neither of us thought God would one day call Olu to invest his gifts there as principal of the school. Before we left, we drove to the center of the campus, which is a bit higher in elevation than the rest of the school, and we saw the refugee camp with a population of about 35,000 people. The Liberian Missionary and Education Convention graciously allowed part of the 1,000-acre campus to be used as a staging area for internally displaced people. Relief agencies maintained the camp, keeping the people fed and ensuring a sufficient water supply.

Upon my return to Liberia in 2006, I was shocked to discover that as many as 1,000 people still lived in the refugee camp on the Ricks campus. These displaced people still had nowhere to go. Some had stopped looking for a place because they lost hope that they would ever leave. Many of the residents are elderly or widowed. Many of the women have birthed children in the camp. The refugee camp is the only home their children have ever known. Most haven't left because they have no family who will help them resettle or they have no land of their own. These people are the poorest of the poor.

While I visited Liberia in 2006 and 2007, God put these refugees on my heart. God made it clear to me that these people were among "the least of these" and that I was called to help. I walked the dirt road toward the refugee camp, known in Liberia as an internal displacement camp, which is located on property owned by the Liberian Baptist Missionary and Education Convention. Ricks Institute is on this same acreage about a quarter of a mile away.

As I walked by the school and into the refugee camp, I met Cecilia Washington. She moved slowly and deliberately, using her cane to navigate the rain-washed road. Not used to seeing a white man walking toward her camp, she stopped and introduced herself and wanted to know who I was. I told her I was the pastor in residence at Ricks Institute and that I had come from America to work with Rev. Olu Menjay for a few weeks. That's when she then told me her name, and we walked together toward the refugee camp.

Mrs. Washington carried her belongings on her head in typical Liberian fashion. It fascinates me how Liberians, mainly women, use their heads for carrying all kinds of objects: water, produce, wood, food, almost anything. Children begin learning this practice soon after they start walking. It's an efficient means of transporting objects. The body uses less energy as weight is distributed through a person's core.

The eyes of Cecelia Washington have seen a lot of suffering. Liberian women are strong, but they age quickly.

Muscles do not become tired as easily, yet this method of transportation is not without costs. Although the women often make it look easy, the constant lifting and carrying takes a toll on their bodies over the years. I've seen women carry objects on their heads while they carry babies bound to their backs and hold other objects in their hands.

I was surprised to learn that Mrs. Washington was only sixty-six years old. Her bent-over frame made her look fifteen years older. When I inquired about the bag she carried on her head, she told me she had been out to find some rice. She had made her way up the road to a neighbor's home to ask for food and had come back with two cups of rice. She was going home to prepare one cup to eat that day and would eat the second cup the next day. Then her cupboard would be bare once again.

Mrs. Washington explained that she was a widow. When I asked if she had children, she told me about her one daughter, Miatta. I had been in the community long enough that I knew Miatta. She was one of the school cooks who lived in the refugee camp. I had already visited Miatta and her family at their home in the camp.

"Miatta is your daughter?" I asked. "She's a wonderful lady!"

"None of my children will help me," Mrs. Washington replied. "They've all gone. There's no one to help me with food except Miatta. She's like a daughter to me."

"So she's not your real daughter, then?"

"No. She's more than a daughter to me!" Mrs. Washington said.

I had met Miatta during my first week of serving as a pastor in residence at Ricks Institute. Abandoned by her husband, she was left to raise several children on her own. Rebels had destroyed her home and church in nearby Krukai Town. She moved into an abandoned brick structure on the Ricks campus but was forced to leave after rebels burned it.

Miatta lived in a stick and mud

Abandoned by her husband, Miatta nevertheless has cared for several elderly women, her own children, and her grandchildren. She lives in the internal displacement camp at Ricks and was hired by Dr. Menjay as one of the school cooks.

hut like the other refugees. She shared sleeping space with all of her children in one room with one bed. Yet in a world driven by greed and selfishness, this woman had a heart as big as the ocean, a smile as wide as the horizon, and a heart that always had room for one more person. In addition to caring for her own children and Mrs. Washington, Miatta had cared for four other widows, including her own mother, until each of them died.

When Rev. Olu Menjay began the feeding program at Ricks, he hired Miatta to cook for the children and faculty. She and her helpers cook rice in huge black cauldrons on a stove built of hardened clay, using bamboo stalks as fuel. It's a hot and physically demanding job. One day as she cooked, I watched as a chicken pecked up a rare piece of scrap food Miatta pitched into the yard. Quickly, another chicken came over to take it away, then another. For the next five minutes, the chicken ran around the yard trying to protect her food, waiting for an opportunity to stop and gulp it down.

Through the civil war, many Liberians lived like these chickens, seeking to take whatever they could find from those around them. Stories of rebels coming into villages and taking what they desired are common. Young boys, brandishing weapons almost as big as they were, took anything they wanted: livestock, food from gardens and homes, personal belongings, anything of value. People hid food and rationed food, and many began to steal food to stay alive. Many forgot about others and lived only for themselves. Stories of children abandoning aging parents were not uncommon.

On a different day, I made my way into the refugee camp and sat with Miatta and Mrs. Washington. I listened to them talk about their lives before the war. They told me how the war changed their lives and how their love for one another grew during the time they spent in the bush (forest). I discovered a bond like that of Ruth and Naomi.

Miatta spoke of the months they lived in the bush when the rebels forced them from their homes. As the group became discouraged and afraid, not knowing how she could keep her children alive, Mrs. Washington told them, "Let's search the Bible and see what it will say to us."

With her Bible open, Mrs. Washington said to me, "This Bible is all that I'm depending on. When I'm walking, I carry this Bible. I read this Bible. I read God's word. Whatever I read in this Bible, I don't believe in anything else but Jesus Christ." Then she looked at her friend Miatta and said, "On earth, here, she's not God, but she's my earthly god; without her I would fall. If I don't praise her name, God would hold me responsible, for she's holding me just like a child."

I understood her point. Miatta was taking care of her. To Mrs. Washington, Miatta was the hands, feet, ears, and eyes of Jesus. Without Miatta's care, Mrs. Washington's suffering might have been too great to bear. Without Miatta, Mrs. Washington would likely have died, as much from lack of love as from lack of food. Mrs. Washington survived the war not only because of Miatta's care but because she had someone to care for. Having another person to care for provided meaning and purpose during a time when nothing seemed to make sense.

With all sincerity, Mrs. Washington smiled and looked at her friend. "Sometimes I be crying," she said. "Tears running down my eyes. She's the only person that comes to comfort me. I have a comforter!" James must have had this picture of Christianity in mind when he wrote, "Religion that God our Father accepts as pure and faultless is this: to look after orphans and widows in their distress and to keep oneself from being polluted by the world" (Jas 1:27, NIV).

Imagine if one in every ten persons in America, or in your state, died. This was the case in the fourteen-year Liberian civil war. After the rebels took over the campus of Ricks Institute, the teachers and students became part of the growing number of people on the move. Varney Sherman, academic supervisor at Ricks, gives an insightful and up-close look at what it's like to be thrust suddenly into a homeless situation. On more than one occasion, he had to find shelter for his family. He offered me a personal account of his encounter with rebel soldiers, a scene that was played out thousands and thousands of times, but with more tragic results:

> One of the many memorable aspects of the Liberian civil war was the massive exodus of people. People were always moving. In most cases, they were moving away from the firings and the indiscriminate shelling of the fighting groups. As they moved away from the fighting areas, they were always confronted with other problems: torture, harassment, and intimidations of all sorts by fighters running away from the front. During the war, my family and I moved so many times.
>
> My wife and I had a brief conference and had agreed not to move again because we had many unpleasant experiences during the last two attacks. However, we packed a few things just in case. At about 10:00 A.M., firing could be heard everywhere. One could hear the air-splitting sound of bullets flying, with people dashing to the ground each time the bullets whistled by. Then a very loud explosion was heard close by that shook the place. Without thinking, we grabbed whatever we could and jumped on the road with thousands of others. LURD [Liberians United for Reconciliation and Democracy] was in Caldwell and we were on the move for the third time in a few days.
>
> It was late in the evening and everybody was beginning to feel the effect of the walk. Then we spotted a village. When we reached it, it was already populated with people who were ahead of us. Given that it was late and the family was tired, I decided we would spend the night there until the next day. About 8:00 P.M., under a heavy downpour, we heard sounds of many footsteps coming from the bush toward us in the village. Before long, we were surrounded by fighters—government troops. There is no way I can give a vivid description of the panic and fear that came over us. Being in a remote village and surrounded by loose fighters meant nothing but torture, harassment, intimidation, and absolute slavery. The panic and fear that ensued as a result of the arrival of the fighters can be gauged only

by the complete quietness that enveloped the entire village the moment they were identified.

"Everybody pack and move immediately!" one of the rebels demanded, but nobody had time to pack. They were already pushing people out in the rain. Dark and wet as it was, we were on the move again. In front of me a lady was sobbing. She had been forced to leave her disabled mother behind. With fighters everywhere and each completely armed, we walked in single file on a snakelike road in total darkness. About midnight, we reached an opening somewhere deep in the forest. Here we were told to stop and rest for the night. After we stopped, the men were separated from the women. I tried to reason why they were doing this, but I could not, at least not at the moment.

It did not take long before I knew what was going on. To the greatest shock of my life, I saw two fighters pass by me carrying two girls who were crying. The girls were virtually being dragged away—sexual harassment! I turned sick immediately. My two daughters were with the others. They were also vulnerable just like the two they took away.

Then I heard the voice of the younger one screaming, telling me that she was being carried away, too. I stepped out from the men's group and faced the man that was pulling her away. He was surprised. He did not think anybody could take such a risk. He was the commander. He asked me what was the matter. I told him the girl was my daughter. "So what?" he said. I told him the girl was very tired from the walks and she needed rest.

He looked at me even more surprised, wondering where I had gotten the courage. He was just a boy. He did not know what it takes to be a father so he could not understand.

Then he pointed his gun at my head and said that if I didn't let the girl go he would fire. I did not know what was going to happen to me, but I was quite resolved in my stand. I responded, "That is the only means by which you will carry her, when I am dead." I was ready to die, withstand any torture, but I was determined not to allow any harm to come to my daughter in my presence.

So the ordeal continued. He beat, slapped, and shoved me around with his gun so many times, but for some reason he never fired. Neither did he order any of his boys to discipline me. At long last, he ordered my daughter and me to sit under a little hut. We sat there, shivering from the rain and the event.

Next, he announced to the group that he was going to kill me and my daughter the next morning as an example to the others. All this while, my wife was crying. In fact, she was wailing, defiant to threats made to her to stop. The rest were dead silent. Fear had cast her spell on them. They were alive, yet dead.

My daughter and I were not killed the next morning. In fact, things changed dramatically. Not a single fighter could be seen when day broke. They had all left under the cover of darkness. So we quietly got on the move again.

This chilling firsthand account demonstrates the trauma the Liberian people constantly endured. Mr. Sherman and his family were fortunate not to be killed by the rebels. Had he not had the courage to stand up for his daughter, she would have been raped and possibly impregnated by the rebel soldiers, as were thousands of other young girls.

In a place like Liberia, one meets plenty of orphans and widows. Especially in a refugee camp, you meet the poorest of the poor. One day, I introduced my work team, Ellen and Farrell Tucker, Pat Tomlinson, and John and Ryan Helms (my sons), to Mrs. Washington. She showed us her house and her garden. We first passed by her old house, which had been claimed by the elements a couple of years earlier: wind, rain, and termites forced her to move into another stick and mud hut. This hut might have lasted for another year or two before the rain washed away the mud and the termites ate away at the small trees, rendering it as useless as the first one. Such houses keep the sun off the people's heads and the rain out only for a while. Eventually the elements win and the people are on the move again.

One thing we all noticed was that Mrs. Washington had placed a lock on her door. A child could have broken into her house, but she put a lock on her door. Even a poor woman in a refugee camp wanted respect. Regardless of her few possessions, she wanted others to respect what she had. She opened the door to allow us to look inside the small one-room house. Her chickens came out before we walked in. It was too dark to see much. What I saw was the concern on Mrs. Washington's face as she showed us her house's deteriorating condition. Who would come to her aid this time?

One night, as I slept under a mosquito net on a comfortable bed in the guest quarters at Ricks Institute, a huge thunderstorm moved through the area. The lightning created momentary shadows on the walls as the trees outside swayed in the wind. The wind was strong enough that the rain began to blow through the windows. I was forced to come out from under my mosquito net and close the glass windows of the guesthouse.

As the storm raged outside, I thought of the refugees in the camp, not more than a mile away. I had first seen that refugee camp in 1995 when Olu and I visited the Ricks campus. At the time, there were 35,000 nameless, faceless people living there.

Ten years later, I knew people in that camp. Most of the people still living in the camp were widows, women, and children. For many like Miatta, their husbands had abandoned them. For others like Mrs. Washington, their husbands had died. An African proverb says a woman without a man is like a field without a seed. Either way, in a land where there are no government agencies to assist the poor, losing the man means additional hardship. These people had nowhere to go and no one to help them establish a home in their old places of residence. Many children were born in the refugee camp and know no other life.

No longer were the people in that camp anonymous and faceless. Now I knew their names, and I knew some of their stories. With the huge storm blowing that night, I began to think about the approaching rainy season and the rickety houses those people inhabited. I could not imagine many of those homes withstanding the elements for another year.

As I listened to the rain, I also began to listen to God. It seemed that God was saying, "If you are so concerned about those refugees living in such terrible conditions, then do something about it." God was trying to get me to move. I immediately thought about the time when Jesus had taught all day. He had tried to move away from the crowds out in the desert, but they found him anyway, thousands of them. Since it was late in the day, the disciples came to Jesus and encouraged him to send the people away so they could go into the villages and buy food. Instead, Jesus told the disciples, "You give them something to eat" (Matt 14:16).

They must have responded with a condescending laugh when they said, "We have here only five loaves of bread and two fish" (v. 17). That's how I felt that night when God spoke to me.

Members of my church had sent money so I could purchase a few bags of cement to help some in the refugee camp finish the floor of their church a few miles away. "How am I supposed to do anything about housing for those refugees?" I wondered. "All I've got is enough money for a few bags of cement."

As the storm died down, I slipped back under the netting. It wouldn't take long before the hot, still, tropical air returned, on which I was sure a malaria-carrying mosquito would come riding. As I lay in bed, I found it difficult to get back to sleep, troubled by God's invitation. As I prayed, I kept asking, "You are joking about the housing thing for the refugees, aren't you?" All I heard was water dripping off the house.

About a week later, I attended the Monrovia Rotary Club meeting.[1] At the Monrovia Rotary Club, I met a man who was in Liberia constructing orphanages. According to UNICEF, the war, along with HIV/AIDS and other diseases, orphaned an estimated 230,000 children. As a retired hospital administrator, this man had found a satisfying job building orphanages. He told me he had searched for a building material that was durable, yet inexpensive. He needed something that could withstand the elements, but these people were extremely poor, so there were few options.

After experiments with building materials, he had found a compressed earth block-making machine that used 90 percent earth and 10 percent cement to produce a brick. Under extremely high pressure, this machine pressed out a brick about twice the size of a regular brick. This brick did not break down in the weather. Structures could be stuccoed or left with a natural brick finish. After the meeting, this builder drove me to a worksite where a house was being constructed with these compressed bricks. The impressive structure stood on cement footers, complete with bricked walls throughout the house.

When I returned to Liberia in 2007, once again I attended a Rotary meeting. This time, an American businessman invited my entire mission team to his Monrovia beach compound. By this time, enough commerce had begun to flow in and out of the city to attract people who knew how to make money. This man had shipped two top-of-the-line compressed earth block-making machines to Liberia. He was in the process of using one of them to build a three-story building across the street from his compound.

I'm slow and hardheaded sometimes. But God had used two different occasions in Liberia to show me a machine that could do the work needed to build permanent housing inexpensively in Liberia. This was what God could use to multiply the dirt and cement and make the building materials necessary for providing housing for the refugees. If this wasn't enough, before I left Liberia in 2007, I received this letter handwritten by Mrs. Washington. Barely literate, this woman wrote to me, pleading for help with a shelter. It was further confirmation that this elderly woman's deepest desire is to have adequate shelter as she ages.

Dear Dr. Helms, Someone to please to gave me some money to built my house. I will surely go back to my town. You yourself went and saw were I am living. It is very bad off. Dr. Machel, you have find you own old lady because I am only depending on Jesus. The only way I can make it is by planing patatoes, greens and sometime begging people to please help me. I want you to please leave your address with me so I can be calling you just so I can hear from you. Please excuse all misstakes. Dr. Machel when you go must please sen me one phone. Please find people the states me and grandchildren so they can go to school. Dr. Machel Helms I which you a save jouney.

Thanks, Mrs. Cecelia M. Washington

I am praying for the day that I will stand in Liberia alongside a house that has been built for Cecelia Washington from bricks produced from a compressed earth block-making machine. Jesus is still on the move, just like these refugees. Jesus is moving me to help people like Mrs. Washington have a safe, secure, durable place to live. Is Jesus moving you too?

Note

1. Rotary is an international service organization made up of more than 1.2 million business, professional, and community leaders. Members of Rotary provide humanitarian service, encourage high ethical standards in all vocations, and help build goodwill and peace in the world. With more than 32,000 Rotary clubs, a Rotarian can find a meeting in most cities throughout the world.

Chapter 16

Come More Often, Lord

The stories I heard, the people I met, and the events I experienced during my trips to Liberia reveal that the world is still a place of unimaginable horrors. However, I also discovered, with great hope, that there are times when kindness can tame savagery. Acts of hospitality, even to those who seem most undeserving, can touch a place in the human heart that a person may not have realized was there. God seeks to create a world in which people live peaceably with each other, loving each other and their God and striving to overcome tremendous need.

Isaiah described a day that is coming:

> The wolf will live with the lamb, the leopard will lie down with the goat, the calf and the lion and the yearling together; and a little child will lead them. The cow will feed with the bear, their young will lie down together, and the lion will eat straw like the ox. The infant will play near the hole of the cobra, and the young child put his hand into the viper's nest. They will neither harm nor destroy on all my holy mountain, for the earth will be full of the knowledge of the LORD as the waters cover the sea. (Isa 11:6-9, NIV)

Such a world, where animalistic instincts give way to peaceful actions, seems light years away, even in America. Amid the carnage of the world, stories of the seniors at Ricks, of people like Miatta and Olu, of groups like the staff at Ricks Institute and the American churches that support the school give us hope. Perhaps we can agree that, in certain bright pockets of the region, God has come fully.

To the people of Liberia, the laws of the jungle seemed like the only laws that existed during their civil war. The war claimed as many as 250,000 lives. It left more than half of Liberia's population homeless, creating a refugee crisis that rivaled any Africa has ever seen. With the raping of women and children, the forced entry of young boys into the rebel army, the indiscriminate looting and killing, people of any faith in God must have cried out, "Come, Lord, come!" We can apply the words of the writer of Genesis to those who fought during the Liberian civil war: ". . . every inclination of the thoughts of his heart was only evil all the time" (Gen 6:5b). As the civilians of Liberia suffered at the mercy of the rebels, the lament rose to God, "Come, Lord, come!"

When President Charles Taylor agreed to go into exile in Nigeria as part of a peace deal and all warring factions agreed to sign a peace agreement stating they would not seek political office, they paved the way for a transitional government and ended the fourteen-year civil war in August 2003. At that time, about 60,000 fighters assimilated back into the population, and another 130,000 people who had been forced to take up arms at some point during the war laid down their weapons. Many of the war's most notorious warlords found refuge in neighboring countries for fear that others might take revenge. With cruel and inhumane acts of violence committed by so many Liberians against their fellow countrymen, the wounds left on the psyche of the Liberian people by this war are deep and wide.

The country needs electricity, running water, debt relief, schools, and the ability to begin exporting natural resources. However, the foundation of any society is peaceful, respectful, and cooperative relationships among its citizens who have equal rights under the law. The greatest challenge facing Liberia today is the rebuilding of relationships between Liberians.

As mentioned earlier, in April 2006, Johnson-Sirleaf emerged from a field of twenty-two candidates to become Liberia's new president, the first female leader of the country and first elected female president on

A woman in the internal displacement camp at Ricks Institute proudly wears clothing made of material that bears the Liberian flag, colors, and image of President Ellen Johnson-Sirleaf.

the continent of Africa. During former dictator Samuel Doe's reign, she was imprisoned twice and was constantly under the threat of rape and execution. A Harvard graduate, Johnson-Sirleaf spoke of healing more than once during her inaugural address: "It is time for us, regardless of our political affiliations or persuasions, to come together, to heal and rebuild our nation."

As a part of this healing process, President Johnson-Sirleaf launched the Liberian Truth and Reconciliation Commission in 2006. It was modeled after one used in South Africa in 1995 after the end of apartheid. In launching the commission, the president said,

> No matter how successful our efforts to establish good governance, the future and the stability of our country will remain in doubt unless we face ourselves as a people, unless we tell the truth of what we did to ourselves and to our nation. . . . There will not be lasting peace nor would there be unity and reconciliation if the truth of our crisis remains the subject of gossip, innuendoes, speculations, assumptions and hearsay. If we fail to take this courageous step at this early period of our nation's renewal, we will only continue to create an environment for the promotion of collective guilt, unfair treatment, uncorroborated accounts of the past and false impression of goodness.[1]

Americans are likely to have many problems with this approach to healing because the commission has no power to try cases. Its only mandate is to "investigate gross human rights violations of international laws as well as abuses that occurred during the war, including massacres, sexual violations, murders, extra-judicial killings and economic crimes."[2] Forgiveness is crucial, but forgiveness without accountability could be a license for people to continue to take advantage of others and use power to oppress and abuse.

Customs in Africa are different from those in America. There are different ways of dealing with conflict and moving through grief. The Truth and Reconciliation Commission is a concept that may be unique to African culture. It gives victims an opportunity to address those who have committed crimes against them. It also gives criminals an opportunity to acknowledge their crimes and ask forgiveness of their victims. The criminal may share information more freely without the threat of prosecution.

Since the information collected by the Truth and Reconciliation Commission cannot be used for prosecution, the main goal is to promote healing. It is a risky endeavor. Instead of healing, for some it may only reopen old wounds, create new ones, or deepen animosity once the truth is known. "In a fragile nation emerging from 14 years of civil war, the Truth and Reconciliation Commission members know that too much rough-edged 'justice' risks igniting backlashes and fresh violence. Yet, too much well-meaning 'mercy' may leave grievances unaddressed, setting the stage for future conflict."[3]

One can usually predict what happens when a lioness and oryx meet face to face; nature will take its course. The oryx will run. It will either get away, or it will be caught and die. But human nature doesn't always follow jungle law. During the Truth and Reconciliation Commission hearings in South Africa, a police sergeant was confronted with some of his atrocities. In one instance, he had taken a man into captivity and shot him at point-blank range in the presence of his wife. In another incident, the sergeant captured the same woman's only son, killed him, and roasted him on a spit like a pig while the officers drank themselves silly. The sergeant admitted to the court that he had done this.

The widow and mother sat in the courtroom. She was asked what she wanted done to the murderer. She said, "I want three things. First, I want the sergeant to know that God forgives him, and so do I. Second, I want him to come to my house one day each week and sit with me because I no longer have anyone for a family. And third, I want to come forward now and hug the sergeant to prove that my love is real." The sergeant fainted, and those in the courtroom quietly began to sing "Amazing Grace."

David Zeren, a professor at Concordia University in Austin, Texas, told this story when he preached at St. Paul's Lutheran Church in Accra, Ghana. When he got to the woman's second wish, the congregation stood on its feet, clapping, shouting, and singing. They knew something of these evils, and they understood why it was important to be free of them. They understood how free this woman felt by throwing aside her need for revenge and accepting God's forgiveness as a gift to be passed on.

That day, God came to the courtroom in South Africa and was later present in the congregation as David Zeren preached. People know it's a rare thing when the lioness lies down with the oryx. People know it's a rare thing when people forgive grave atrocities. Whenever a radical repositioning of the heart happens, God has come.

I witnessed this in Liberia when I sat and spoke with families of teenage boys whom the rebels had forced to become soldiers. The leaders of these rebels violated international law, forcing young boys to depend on them for their lives in exchange for brandishing a machine gun and killing on demand, but in Liberia during the civil war, the only law was the law of the jungle. Even though these boys were taken from their homes, drugged, and taught to kill, when the war ended, many simply laid down their weapons and walked back to their families. The ones I met were not disowned. Instead, they were welcomed home. The families knew these boys were survivors and also victims and didn't view them as killers.

For too long, the people of Liberia have been a fractured people. Heritage, class, prejudices, tribes, and education levels have divided them. Now that Liberia has imploded and is in the process of picking up the pieces, perhaps her citizens will not be so easily led astray by uneducated people who promise what they cannot deliver.

I am hopeful that the Truth and Reconciliation Commission can do much good for the country. It is true that the vast majority of the people who committed great atrocities against Liberians will never be brought to justice. Ironically, one of the greatest perpetrators of all, former President Charles Taylor, may never have charges brought against him from his own country; but he faces crimes against the people of Sierra Leone from the War Crimes Tribunal at The Hague, Netherlands. These may keep him in prison for the rest of his life.

I was in Liberia on Monday, March 27, 2006, when Charles Taylor disappeared from the southern Nigerian villa where he had been exiled since the peace treaty was signed. The Nigerians were not holding him under tight security, so when he heard that the political winds had shifted and newly elected President Ellen Johnson-Sirleaf was going to ask Nigeria to hand him over, he escaped. Only loosely guarded, he essentially drove away.

Taylor stood accused by the international community of destabilizing the government of Sierra Leone in order to capture their diamond trade. His rebel soldiers were notorious for hacking off the hands and legs of civilians during their decade-long war. The announcement in Monrovia of his sudden disappearance spread like wildfire. There was noticeable anxiety on people's faces as they gathered around battery-operated radios to listen to news. It was as if they had heard that an approaching army was headed their way. Could this man gather another group of rebels and take away the peace and hope that had finally come to their land?

Fortunately, it ended a day later. Taylor was arrested attempting to cross the boarder into Cameroon. He drove a Land Rover and carried huge amounts of cash. The mood in Monrovia shifted from one of fear to one of celebration. On Wednesday, a United Nations helicopter flew Taylor back to Liberia. On previous occasions he had used overtones about being a preacher. His return to Liberia might have been the closest he'd come to fulfilling prophetic words. As he surrendered power and gave up the presidency in 2003, he had said, "God willing, I will return."

He returned only briefly. He barely had time to set foot on Liberian soil and feel the warm breeze blowing in from the Atlantic before being handed over to United Nations Peacekeepers who flew him to Sierra Leone to face a war crimes tribunal. In order to ensure a fair trial and to ensure that the region was not destabilized in any way by Taylor's presence, he was eventually moved to The Hague. He should no longer be a threat to Liberia.

In a twisted way, Taylor might have contributed to Liberia's becoming a more homogeneous people. During the war, people from all parts of Liberia ended up in Monrovia, causing the city to double in size. The city became a safe haven as people left the hinterland and the surrounding areas of Monrovia seeking to escape the rebels. Monrovia became a melting pot of people groups from all over the country. Because of this, intermarriage between Americo-Liberians and indigenous/Congo people has occurred. With each passing generation, the lines between people groups will grow less and less prominent.

Will Liberia emerge from this crisis as one nation, or will it continue to be a nation divided? Will the people learn to embrace one another as fellow Liberians regardless of their heritage? Will the government make sure all Liberians are treated equally and represented fairly in government?

One can find emerging signs of hope in unusual places. Most of the time, people don't care which vine bears the fruit of hope. As long as hope is not false, as long as hope has a firm foundation, and as long as hope is not contrary to the love of God, we shouldn't be concerned about how hope is packaged.

Richard Duo has found hope in an unusual place, but before I tell you where he found it, let me tell you where he lost it. Richard was four years old when Samuel Doe's men entered St. Peter's Lutheran Church, where children and their mothers had gathered for refuge in the Sinkor area of Monrovia, Liberia. These people believed that within the confines of a holy sanctuary, they would be safe from rebel soldiers. They were not. A soldier cut off Richard's leg with a sword and left him to die with 600 others.

Richard survived, but as an amputee in a third-world country, his life has been difficult. Although Richard never fought for the rebels, he is often mistaken for a fighter because of his amputation. While most fighters from this war have blended into the population, amputees are easily identified as casualties; most of them are ex-militia. Hundreds of amputees throughout Liberia are easy targets for people to vent their anger regarding the raping, pillaging, and murdering rebels committed at the commands of their leaders.

Although innocent of these things, Richard has, nonetheless, caught the wrath of many. In addition, he suffers the same plight of other amputees: no available prosthesis and no available job. Richard is left with the only survival technique known to many like him in a third-world country—begging.

A couple of years ago, a preacher came to the amputees with a message of hope. He told them that their amputations did not remove God's purpose from their lives. He quoted words from the book of Jeremiah: "'For I know the plans I have for you,' declares the LORD, 'plans to prosper you and not to harm you, plans to give you hope and a future'" (Jer 29:11, NIV).

This preacher did more than simply quote Scripture about hope. He planted hope among the amputees on a soccer field. The Reverend had heard how the game of soccer had brought hope to amputees in neighboring Sierra Leone, a place that had also experienced a recent civil war.

While it seems strange to think of amputees playing soccer, the love for the game has restored self-respect to these men. With amazing agility, they race across the field aided by arm crutches. Hoisting their bodies upward, they launch the ball toward a goal protected by a one-armed man. More amazing than their ability to overcome their physical handicaps is their willingness to overcome their deep emotional wounds to play this game. In some cases, men who once opposed each other on the battlefield wear the same jersey. Sometimes, men like Richard, an innocent bystander and casualty of the war, team with men who committed savage crimes against local communities. People even come to watch these men square off against one another in competition and cheer their progress. As they do, the amputees gain new respect from the same people who have judged them for the crimes many of them committed.

Part of finding hope for the future is learning to build on the present. Of course, like Richard Duo, we are not always given the present we desire, and none of us can change our past. Nevertheless, we each have decisions to make about the future we want to create. The future of Liberia depends greatly on how people choose to interact with those who have mistreated and wounded one another. In America, the North and South had to learn to get along after the American Civil War. The people of Liberia must do the same. They do not have the liberty of being divided by region. They are face to face with each other every day.

The Truth and Reconciliation Commission in Liberia can help the people by giving the country a healthy sense of self-awareness. Just as self-awareness is important to being a healthy person and family, it is also important for a nation. Through an understanding of where they have been and some awareness of what they must do to get where they need to go, the Liberian people can sustain hope. Hope must stay alive for abundant life to occur. Any time we find redeeming hope, God has come.

Joan D. Chittister calls this the "gift of conversion. . . . Conversion is the opening of the heart to the grace of new possibilities. It does not blame God for plotting nefarious plans to test and try and torment us. It recognizes in the glory of new life that God simply companions us. He simply stands by ready to receive our tattered, restless selves as we are tested, tried, and tormented by the machinations of life itself. God guides us to new life by allowing us to open our eyes to possibility and find it for ourselves."[4]

Jesus taught us to work and to pray for the ushering in of God's kingdom, even as evil persists and even as we understand that God's kingdom will not be fully realized until the Second Advent of Christ. Perhaps God will come through Liberia's new leader, President Johnson-Sirleaf. Perhaps God will come through Liberians like Dr. Olu Menjay who return there to invest in Liberian children, helping them find hope through education. Perhaps God will come through Liberia's Truth and Reconciliation Commission. Perhaps God will come through the common people of Liberia, people who have suffered but have not forsaken God. Perhaps God will come through Liberia's children and youth, who have seen enough war that they will do everything in their power to maintain peace in the generations to come. Perhaps God will come through you, a person who is moved to become involved in some way to bring hope to those who struggle day by day, helping them to pick up the pieces of their society and rebuild.

If Liberia's people listen to one another and begin to love one another, God will come. If the lioness is to lie down with the oryx, there must be more understanding than blame, more unity than division, more steps toward the future than angry retreats into the past, a willingness to listen and not a desire to accuse, and a true desire to confess sin and move toward reconciliation.

In order for us to help countries like Liberia and even our own, we all must be willing to acknowledge the sins of our past, learn from them, and vow not to repeat them. I hope our moral compass has moved far enough toward respecting human rights of all humankind that our country can fully live out her motto, "*E Pluribus Unum*," Out of Many One. More importantly, for Christians, I hope we can learn to live out the two greatest commands of the Bible: "Love the Lord your God with all your heart and with all your soul and with all your mind" (Matt 22:37), and "Love your neighbor as yourself" (Matt 22:39). If everyone lived with these two commandments as life's mantra, wars would cease, and there would be hope for Liberia, hope for America, and hope for the world.

I wrote this book because I want to do my small part to *hope* Liberians as they move into the future. After I saw the refugees at Ricks Institute, worshiping with Liberians in their churches, spending time in the classroom with the students and following them to their homes, the words of James haunted me like a shadow. I couldn't simply say to those people, "Go, I wish you well; keep warm and well fed" (Jas 2:16) and do nothing about their physical needs.

As we help the people of Liberia get back on their feet and encourage them to see every Liberian as significant in the eyes of God, we can hope that, one day, we might see all Liberians embracing like Jacob and Esau and prospering like them as well. Until then, Liberia remains a broken, hungry, illiterate, disease-ridden, mostly jobless land. Yet she is not without hope.

Jeremiah's words of hope to the Jews exiled in Babylon seem appropriate for the people of Liberia: "'For I know the plans I have for you,' declares the LORD, 'plans to prosper you and not to harm you, plans to give you hope and a future'" (Jer 29:11, NIV).

Before leaving Liberia in 2006, I asked Rev. Menjay to drive our team to the beach at the ELWA radio station in Paynesville. I wanted to see the coconut palm trees planted by the missionary in 1995. The trees had grown about ten feet. I stood on the beach and remembered being told by the missionary how hundreds of trees were cut down so the people could eat the tree's cabbage and keep from starving. These new trees were not planted for food. They were planted for hope, to remind the people that they were people with a future. Just like those trees, hope was growing.

I left Liberia with the belief that Liberia's best days are yet to come. I invite you to join me and many others as we continue the work of so many who have come before us in *Hoping Liberia*.

Please join me in praying, "Come more often, Lord! Come more often!"

Notes

1. Jonathan Paye-Layleh, "Liberia President officially launches post-conflict Truth and Reconciliation Commission," AP Worldstream news release, 22 June 2006.

2. Ibid.

3. Abraham McLaughlin, "Mercy vs. justice as Liberia heals itself: Liberia's new Truth and Reconciliation Commission seeks a balance between punishment and forgiveness," *Christian Science Monitor* (26 October 2006), http://www.csmonitor.com/2006/1026/p12s01-woaf.html.

4. Joan D. Chittister, *Scarred by Struggle, Transformed by Hope* (Grand Rapids: Eerdmans Publishing Company, 2003) 25.

Dr. Olu Menjay and Dr. Michael Helms on the beach with the city of Monrovia, a city on a hill, set in the background.

Epilogue

This story illustrates the amazing resilience of the Liberian people. Many innocent people were brutally murdered during the successive waves of fighting from December 24, 1989, until the war ended fourteen years later. Thousands found refuge in neighboring countries: Sierra Leone, Guinea, Ivory Coast, Ghana, and Nigeria. The fortunate were granted political asylum in the United States. Many people were driven from their homes, leaving their possessions behind at least twice and sometimes more often. When others might have given up hope, many Liberians held on to their hope for a better day and slowly set out to rebuild after each wave of destruction.

When I saw the Ricks campus in early 1991, I wondered how it could survive such destruction. The library/administration building had been bombed. Other buildings were seriously damaged; all equipment and supplies were looted, and most of the staff was forced to flee. In three subsequent visits, I shed tears over the pitiful appearance of the campus and the abortive efforts to get the school running again.

Our all-knowing and all-seeing God was even then preparing a new leader to provide the vision and hope necessary for reviving this historic and prestigious educational institution. Olu Menjay had not sought the job as principal of Ricks Institute; the job sought him. It was a major and difficult decision, and Olu sought the counsel of friends and the leadership of God in accepting the challenge of leading the school.

Olu's winsome personality resulted in contacts with many influential and resourceful people who have played a big part in the Ricks revival. Teams of workers from churches and schools have invested heavily by repairing the facilities, providing leadership seminars for teachers and area pastors, and obtaining new equipment for the kitchen, dining hall, dormitories, administration building, clinic, and farming program.

As God used Olu Menjay to lead the resurgence of Ricks Institute, so God continues to use him in the further development of Ricks and in innovative methods of education in the Liberian culture. It is refreshing that this initiative has not been bound by a "business as usual" mentality. Challenges and difficulties loom large when a ministry of this magnitude is undertaken. There is a constant necessity to address land boundary disputes and the selfish requests of those who benefit most from such an institution.

Olu Menjay has now completed requirements for a Ph.D degree from the University of Wales through the International Baptist Theological Seminary in Prague. He is to be congratulated for his perseverance and dedication that has brought him to this peak of achievement.

All readers are aware of the worldwide economic crisis. This makes it more urgent that interested friends make a special effort to provide adequate funding and assistance to ensure the uninterrupted effectiveness of Ricks Institute.

One can hope Olu Menjay's example motivates and challenges many other Liberians who presently live in the States. Some have received excellent education and experience that has equipped them to give desperately needed leadership in the rebuilding of Liberia. Liberia has an urgent need for its citizens living abroad to return home and invest themselves in the rebuilding of their country. Their presence can make a huge difference.

The Bricks for Ricks Liberian Housing Foundation, Inc., is a practical and profitable concept. The compressed bricks made from 90 percent laterite soil and 10 percent cement are solid and durable. In 1965, I built an entire campus for a Pastor's Training School in Sinoe County, Liberia, out of compressed bricks (dirt bricks in some places). Forty-four years later, these walls still stand. These bricks reduce the cost of building a house by a big percent and result in a durable structure.

We feel deep gratitude to Dr. Michael Helms for his interest and investment in Liberia. *Hoping Liberia—Stories of Civil War from Africa's First Republic* is a well-written and accurate book on the history of Liberia and the outstanding work of Dr. Olu Menjay and Ricks Institute. Through reading this book, may you be encouraged to invest in this great ministry.

—Rev. John Mark Carpenter
President Emeritus, Liberian Baptist Theological Seminary
Liberian Missionary (1961–1977; 1983–1993)

Hoping Small Groups
Questions for Reflection and Discussion

Chapter 1

1. Name some qualities that have made America a great nation.

2. Has America lost much of her good name in the eyes of the world? Defend your answer.

3. Name a time when you have used someone else's name as a reference or to network. Who was that person? Why did you choose that person and how did the good name of the person help you?

4. What does it take to be known as a person with a good name?

5. Discuss Proverbs 22:1: "A good name is more desirable than great riches; to be esteemed is better than silver or gold" (NIV).

6. What role does memory play in the establishment of a good name? Talk about this from a positive perspective. Talk about this from a negative perspective.

Chapter 2

1. After such events as the American slave trade, the Trail of Tears, and the Jewish Holocaust, we should always be aware of the danger that exists when people espouse claims of superiority over other groups. Can you give examples where groups today claim superiority over other groups? If so, what danger do you see in these actions? Has conflict already developed?

2. Do you agree that there is a connection between the 14-year civil war in Liberia and the slave trading days in the United States. Why or why not?

3. Can you recall a time in biblical history or in general history when people repeated mistakes of previous generations?

4. Are there examples from your own family history in which a family member repeated his or her mistakes?

5. What do you make of the fact that Christians were heavily involved in establishing a colony for freed slaves? What motivated these Christians?

6. The phrase "all men are created equal" is a part of the Declaration of Independence, yet America was a slaveholding nation. Why did this inconsistency exist?

7. Why did Caldwell believe if the concepts that "all men are created equal" and all have "unalienable rights" were applied to the freed slaves, hope among whites would be destroyed?

8. Do you see evidence of Manifest Destiny in America today? Do some people believe that America is God's chosen nation, the "new people of Israel"? Has America developed an arrogant attitude toward people of other countries? Defend your answer.

9. Discuss these statements: "The American Colonization Society is a reminder that just because a movement is born in the church doesn't make it Christian. Just because an organization or idea has the support of many Christians, it may still not be Christian."

10. Despite the motives of those who worked to establish the colony for freed slaves on the shores of West Africa, did freed slaves arrive there with hope? Did they begin new lives there with hope?

Chapter 3

1. We know that God speaks to us through Scripture and prayer. What other ways does this chapter suggest that God speaks to us?

2. Have you ever had the shock of adjusting to another culture? What would it be like to arrive in a foreign country and have to adjust to that country's language, customs, laws, food, and religion? Can you think of any examples in the Bible where people had to do this?

3. This chapter suggests that God goes before us to prepare the way for us to do things He wants us to do. Can you give some biblical examples? Can you share some personal examples?

4. Are you prone to dismiss ideas as being impossible or impractical without consulting God or without considering that God is still in the business of making the improbable a reality?

5. Holding onto a letter changed the author's life. Had he thrown it away, he would have never made a trip to Liberia with Dr. Menjay or written this book. The small decisions we make every day are important. Can you share a little decision that changed your life? How often do we ask God to help us in the small choices we make every day?

6. Discuss this sentence from the end of this chapter: "When we are obedient to God's guidance, we are not always given a clear reason we are being asked to do something. Sometimes, it's weeks, months, or years later before we are able to look back and see how God's plan unfolded in our lives. We may have to have the perspective of heaven before we know the reasons for many of the things we are asked to do."

Chapter 4

1. Highly recommended: Watch the movie *Amazing Grace* (dir. Michael Apted, 2006). This is an excellent film based on the true story of the British politician William Wilberforce, who was converted to Christianity, resulting in major changes in his life, including his conviction that the slave trade should be abolished. Instead of becoming a minister, he was convinced by others that he could be of more use to God's kingdom by remaining an activist in Parliament. His tireless and costly campaign against the British slave trade led to the eventual passage of a law that abolished the practice in 1807. *Amazing Grace* highlights the influence former slave trader John Newton had on Wilberforce's life and how his song "Amazing Grace" influenced Wilberforce's life.

Suggestions for small group discussion:

• Watch scene 10; it describes the brutal conditions mentioned in this chapter of how slaves were transported from Africa to America.
• Watch Wintley Phipps's history and performance of the song "Amazing Grace" on YouTube at http://www.youtube.com/watch?v=DMF_24cQqT0 &feature=related. Discuss what you've seen and heard in these two clips.

2. Discuss Reverend Robert Walsh's description of the transportation of slaves aboard ships in the early 1800s.

3. Does it surprise you that the Southern Baptist Convention was formed over the issue of slavery in 1845? What warning(s) should this fact give to modern Christians?

4. Why is false hope a dangerous thing?

Chapter 5

1. Have you ever experienced culture shock? Describe it to the group.

2. Have you ever experienced meaningful worship in a setting with different traditions and unfamiliar liturgy? Describe that experience. If not, speculate why you have not.

3. What does it mean to "embody hope" for someone else? For whom do you embody hope? Who looks to you for hope?

4. Discuss the statement, "Hope rides on the updraft of those we join in Christian formation." (see appendix 3)

5. Recall a story from Scripture or a personal story that gives hope to your life.

6. Have you ever had a time in your life when you've doubted parts of your Christian faith? How did you move through your doubt?

7. Tell of a time when you have had hope renewed in you when you least expected it.

Chapter 6

1. According to freed slave Peyton Skipworth, was the colony becoming successful?

2. Compare the similarities and differences between the relationships of the freed slaves and the tribesmen (indigenous people of West Africa) to the relationships of the settlers from England who immigrated to the New World and the American Indians (the indigenous people of the New World).

3. After being oppressed for many years in America, why do you think the Americo-Liberians became oppressors?

4. Even though things improved under the presidency of William Tubman, how did his one-party democracy continue to contribute to the frustrations and undercurrent of disenfranchisement of the indigenous people?

Chapter 7

1. God placed a rainbow in the sky after the Great Flood. At ELWA radio station in Paynesville, Liberia, a missionary planted a row of coconut palm trees on the beach after refugees cut down and ate the insides of the ones that used to be there. How did the newly planted palms trees represent hope? What signs of hope do you see around you?

2. Do you believe God put a hedge around the library at the Liberian Baptist Theological Seminary? If so, why would God protect some things and not others from the attack of the rebels?

3. Choose one or more of these statements for discussion.

• When love abounds, there is no specific gestation period for hope.
• If we see no evidence of hope, then hope has died.
• Hope is harder to kill than kudzu (kudzu is a vine in the South that grows several feet a day in the summer and covers trees, buildings, and even many acres of land).

4. What did the Exile teach the Jews about hope and worship?

5. Where is hope evident at First Baptist Clay?

6. "God can just sling seeds to the wind, but most of the time God's looking for someone to sow seeds of hope. He's looking for someone to say, 'Here I am, Lord. Send me.'" Where might God want you to go as an individual or your church to go to plant seeds of hope?

Chapter 8

1. Why is self-awareness critical for hope? Have you ever been so close to a situation that you could not see an issue until you backed away? Even though President Tolbert was a Christian, what couldn't he see that cost him his presidency and perhaps his life? With the brief sketch of the issues given, what self-awareness do you think he lacked? What self-awareness did Samuel Doe lack?

2. Consider further researching Gabriel Baccus Matthews. Could he have become a Martin Luther King, Jr. figure in Liberia? What prevented that?

3. What was significant about Samuel Doe's presidency? Did it solve any of the people's problems? What did the assassination of the president and then the assassination of Doe do for the hope of the country?

Chapter 9

1. In the movie *Forrest Gump*, Forrest's friend Jenny returns home. As they walk through the countryside, they come to the old house where Jenny lived as a child. It was in that house that her father sexually abused her. When Jenny sees the house, dangerous memories return. She begins picking up rocks and throwing them at the house until she can't find any more. She falls to her knees and weeps. Forrest says, "Sometimes, there's just not enough rocks."

For those willing to risk something personal from your past, what memories do you struggle with? If you trust your group, they might help you find some rocks.

2. When is anger righteous, propelling God's people to stand up against evil? When does anger cross the line and become sin? Which kind of anger did the psalmist have in Psalm 137? What anger did Dr. Menjay deal with in Liberia?

3. Have people ever looked to you to provide more than you were capable of providing?

4. The book of Lamentations was composed soon after the destruction of Jerusalem in 586 BC. Jerusalem is lying in ruins and people from the city have been carried off into exile.

Many of the psalms, called psalms of lament, express grief and a lack of understanding. At times the writer of a lament boldly questions God and cries out to God for answers. Psalm 74 is an example of a communal lament. Psalm 55 is an example of an individual lament. Choose one of these or another psalm of lament. Read it and discuss some of its elements. What surprises you about the way the psalmist speaks to God? Why is the lament a healthy part of the psalmist's faith?

5. If you had to write a psalm of lament, what would it be about? Where are grief, sorrow, and brokenness in your life right now? Do you think God understands? Do you think others understand?

6. Read the following paragraph.

"Memories can be dangerous because they tend to show us that our faith in God isn't black and white. Faith isn't simple. Faith is a mixture of assurances and doubts, a mixture of promises that have been fulfilled and others that have yet to be. It is the courage of allowing memory to be one's teacher, which can be scary and unsettling. If we allow memory to take us by the hand and carry us where we've come from, we might learn things about ourselves we did not want to learn. If we continue to walk into the future to meet God, God can take our memories and use them 'together for good.' When we allow God to use memories to enhance our faith, God can unlock fetters from around us as we deal with the negative issues from our past and affirm everything in our past that's blessed us, catapulting us into the future where God already exists."

Which parts of the paragraph do you agree with? With which do you disagree? How has God used memory to enhance your faith? How can memory work as an enemy? If we get locked into the past, how can God deliver us and help us move into the future?

Chapter 10

1. Ministers are not the only people who feel called to a vocation. Considering the amount of time we spend working over a lifetime, shouldn't we all feel a sense of call to the vocation we have? Why or why not?

2. Rev. Harrison Menjay presented Olu with a new Bible at his ordination and quoted Luke 2:29-30, "Lord, now lettest thou thy servant depart in peace, according to thy word: for mine eyes have seen thy salvation" (KJV). Do you think he had a premonition that his life might be coming to an end? Do you ever think about your own death? It's not a comfortable subject, is it? Have you ever been in a near death situation? If so, did that experience change the way you live?

3. At your funeral, what kinds of things would you want the minister to say about your life?

4. Dr. Menjay used Psalm 1:3 for his father's eulogy: "He was like a tree planted by streams of water." What text would you like to be used for your eulogy?

5. Have you ever been shaken by a death? Tell about that experience. How did that person's death change you?

6. Has death caused you to have a crisis of faith?

Chapter 11

1. Define success as typically defined in America or by the world's standards.

2. Define success as you think God defines it.

3. Do we make it to heaven based on success? Is abundant life, as defined by Jesus, based on success or is it based on something else? If so, what?

4. This chapter discussed a difference between living a life of success as defined by the world and living a life of significance. What is the difference? Can both be achieved?

5. Who has most strongly influenced your life?

6. In Dr. Olu Menjay's search for living a life of significance, where did he ultimately find it?

7. Discuss Deuteronomy 8:17-18: "You may say to yourself, 'My power and the strength of my hands have produced this wealth for me.' But remember the LORD your God, for it is he who gives you the ability to produce wealth, and so confirms his covenant, which he swore to your forefathers, as it is today." (NIV)

8. This chapter challenges readers to discover their gifts and to use their gifts to help others in need as a step toward living a significant life. What are you currently doing to help someone in need? As a result of this study, you may want to pray and ask God to lead you to a person or a ministry

where your gifts are needed. Your group may decide to pool resources and do a joint project of significance. What are some things you might do?

Chapter 12

1. The fact that the richest fifth of the world's population consumes 86 percent of the world's resources shows us how poor most of the world is—or perhaps how greedy the top fifth is. We work hard to acquire what we have. Then we spend much of our time trying to keep what we have. Instead of *having* possessions, we allow our possessions to *have* us. For many people, the driving force in life becomes the things money buys, then the work required to buy more things. It's a never ending cycle. How do you know when your possessions have you, instead of you having your possessions?

2. It takes money to fund mission efforts around the world. However, the examples of this chapter do not simply focus on money needed to help Ricks; they emphasize the formation of relationships. Recall the different kinds of relationships that have developed with the school. How are lives being changed on both sides of the ocean because of those relationships?

3. Discuss the current mission philosophy of Southern Baptists that has turned away from sending missionaries with such occupations as doctors, nurses, agriculturists, and teachers in order to win the right to share the gospel and instead sends missionaries into countries with an immediate mandate to evangelize.

4. If someone from a foreign country visited your church, whose picture near your church or in your church do you think they would be interested in taking? What story would they take home to tell?

5. Despite their poverty, Liberians can be very giving people. Have you ever been humbled by the generosity of someone whom you knew could not afford to give you a gift?

6. If you are studying this book in a small group, have each participant bring a photograph that has a special significance and share its meaning. What photographs do you carry with you all the time? Why do we carry photographs with us?

7. There is a rhythm to life. We need familiarity to bring us comfort. What is there in your life that is familiar and comfortable to you right now?

8. Change is inevitable. Change is part of life. Measured change, mixed in with familiar settings, is good. However, people often resist most forms of change, even good change. Why? When can the resistance to change become unhealthy?

9. What amazes you about how God's world is ordered?

10. How do you think the people of Liberia have experienced rhythm and change as they have moved through civil war and now through this emerging time of peace?

Chapter 13

1.Have you ever been in a situation where you needed to be rescued?

2. Agree or disagree with the following statement: "The biggest difference between most people, American or foreign born, is opportunity."

3. How do you think you would respond if you were to get a letter from a refugee (someone you had met on a previous occasion) asking for help to come to America to escape the poverty and hopelessness of his/her existence and receive an education in an American college?

4. Have you ever felt God speaking to you? What was the situation? What did you sense God telling you to do? What did you do? What was the outcome?

5. Name some biblical stories where God spoke to people and gave them tasks to accomplish.

6. Have you ever started out on a venture with God that other people thought was foolish?

7. What parts of the stories of Henry Peabody and Dorris Seh speak to you and challenge you in your own walk with the Lord as you seek to listen to God and minister to others?

8. What promise did God keep with the author? What promises has God kept with you?

Chapter 14

1. Talk about the juxtaposition of the graves of the missionary and the rebel soldier buried on the campus. What do you think were the differences in their worldviews?

2. Only three generations after the freed slaves landed on the Western shores of Africa and two years after Liberia became the first republic of Africa, Moses Ricks had a vision for Liberia's future that involved education and faith. Talk about the significance of this man's gift. Place it in the context of his day and ours.

3. We all enjoy the shade of trees we did not plant. What future needs do you see in your church or community that someone needs to address? Have a little fun here. If you or your group were given $500,000 or $1,000,000 to invest for kingdom causes that would have the most impact for future generations, what would you do?

4. Do all dreams for the kingdom have to begin with money? If not, what do other dreams need?

5. The author mentions verses from James 2 several times. "If one of you says to him, 'Go, I wish you well; keep warm and well fed,' but does nothing about his physical needs, what good is it? In the same way, faith by itself, if it is not accompanied by action, is dead" (Jas 2:15-17 NIV). What points is he trying to make by using such verses alongside these stories from Liberia?

6. What everyday things do we take for granted that are considered luxuries in Liberia? How do you think you would live without these?

7. How do you reconcile Matthew 25:32-43 with Ephesians 2:8-10?

Chapter 15

1. Find out which person in the group has moved the most number of times.

• Who has moved when you didn't want to move? Tell the group about the experience.

• Has anyone been forced to move without having a place to go? What did that feel like? If you haven't, what do you think that would feel like?

2. Describe the relationship between Miatta and Mrs. Washington. Have you encountered other relationships like this one? Explain.

3. We've seen people on the move in natural disasters: fires and earthquakes in California, hurricanes on the Gulf coast, floods throughout the country. Is our nation compassionate during these times? What about other times?

4. Where do you see God moving in the world? Where is God moving in your life?

5. Discuss Acts 17:28a, "For in him we live and move and have our being." What does the Apostle Paul mean by this?

6. When God is on the move, it's not unusual for God to take a little and multiply it into a lot. Have you seen this happen in your life? How do you think this might happen with the Bricks for Ricks project? Will you close by praying for God to continue to bless this project for the sake of the refugees and students at Ricks Institute?

Chapter 16

1. When have you witnessed kindness disarm a violent situation or a combative person?

2. Do you see God as a God of wrath or a God of grace? Since Jesus is our best picture of the nature of God, what perspective does Jesus add to the previous question?

3. When evil runs rampant, does the silence of God test your faith? What contributions does Joan Chittister's definition of "gift of conversion" bring to this question?

4. What do you think of the Liberian Truth and Reconciliation Commission? What are its strengths and weaknesses?

5. When you hear someone testify that "God has come" in his/her life, are you skeptical, or are you one who tends to have little doubt about people's stories of encounters with God?

6. Name different ways that God comes to people. Share how God has come to you recently. How did this change your outlook or your life?

7. How did God come to people in Scripture? Does God come to people the same today or differently?

8. How has the study of this book changed you or your walk with Christ? How has the participation in this group study made a difference in how you live the Christian faith?

9. Consider writing the author a note or writing Dr. Olu Menjay to share how God is using his story and the stories of this book to hope you in your journey of faith. Letters to Dr. Olu Menjay, Sr. can be addressed to the same address, in care of Dr. Helms.

Dr. Michael Helms
First Baptist Church
81 Institute Street
Jefferson, GA 30549

Appendix 1:
Bricks for Ricks

Bricks for Ricks Liberian Housing Foundation, Inc., was founded in October 2008. All royalties from this book, as well as any donations, go to help relocate refugees who still live on the campus of Ricks Institute, assist in the educational enhancements of Ricks Institute, and educate young Liberians by equipping them to be the hope for Liberia's future. This is done in the spirit of Ricks Institute's Motto: "Not for Self, but for Others."

Bricks for Ricks has a functioning board that has adopted a policy of financial openness to all who partner with us in our goals of helping the refugees and the students of Ricks Institute. Financial statements will be sent to all donors who make such a request.

The first and main priority of the foundation is to purchase a compound earth brick-making machine, which makes bricks from 90 percent earth and 10 percent cement. This brick does not break down in the Liberian elements, is inexpensive to produce, and results in a structure that can be passed down to the next generation. Machines vary in size and cost.

Since the amount of money required to purchase a brick-making machine is substantial and will take time to acquire, we have chosen the WMU Foundation to manage our money. The Woman's Missionary Union has partnered with Ricks Institute and is interested in rekindling "a passion for God's mission among God's people." That makes partnering with their foundation an easy choice for us in housing our money. Their philosophy matches ours. As you partner with us, the WMU Foundation will ensure that the money will grow safely but steadily until we reach our goal.

A website, http://bricksforricks.org, has been established to inform, educate, and update those interested in the plight of those still living in the internal displacement camp at Ricks Institute. The site contains pictures and personal stories of those living in the camp as well as updates of the author's progress toward purchasing brick-making machines (made possible by book sales and donations) and building permanent housing for these people in their former villages. This website will also provide other useful information about Ricks Institute and its principal, Dr. Olu Menjay.

You have helped by purchasing *Hoping Liberia—Stories of Civil War from Africa's First Republic.* The more books you purchase, the more you help. You can also help by sending a donation to our foundation. All donations will be acknowledged.

Make checks payable to:
Bricks for Ricks Foundation

Mail checks to:
Jefferson First Baptist Church
81 Institute Street
Jefferson, Georgia 30549

Appendix 2:
Ricks Institute

Visit the Ricks Institute website: www.ricksonline.org. The website maintains current information on the school's admission process, academic requirements, campus life, need for volunteers, and ways to partner with the school in mission projects. You will also find information about Ricks Board of Advisors and a special link to the Ricks Alumni Association.

In the 2008–2009 school year, $400 is all that it takes to pay for the complete education of a student at Ricks Institute. An investment in a student at Ricks is an investment in the healing and the future of Liberia.

If you'd like to give money directly to Ricks Institute, you can do so online through WorldWideWord, Inc. If you want to give directly by mail, you can make a tax-deductible gift of $100 or more to Ricks Institute by check or money order payable to:

WorldWideWord, Inc.
c/o David Rochester
24162 Rochester Lane
Aldie, VA 20105

Please indicate on the check's memo line: Ricks Institute, Liberia

(WorldWideWord, Inc. does not charge Ricks Institute for the transfer of funds.)

Further Reading

"Aboard a Slave Ship, 1829." *EyeWitness to History*, www.eyewitnesstohistory.com. 2000.

Archibald, Alexander. *A History of Colonization on the Western Coast of Africa*. Philadelphia: W. S. Martien, 1846.

Barnes, W. W. *The Southern Baptist Convention 1845–1953*. Nashville: Broadman Press, 1953.

Brundage, William Fitzhugh. *Where These Memories Grow: History, Memory, and Southern Identity*. Chapel Hill: University of North Carolina Press, 2000.

Carmichael, Mary. "An Irrepressible Idea." *Newsweek* (19 January 2004), http://www.newsweek.com/id/52790.

Cheatham, Melvin. *Living a Life that Counts*. Nashville: Thomas Nelson Publishers, 1995.

Chittister, Joan D. *Scarred by Struggle, Transformed by Hope*. Grand Rapids: Eerdmans Publishing Company, 2003.

Clegg, Claude A. III. *The Price of Liberty: African Americans and the Making of Liberia*. Chapel Hill: University of North Carolina Press, 2004.

Ellis, Stephen. *The Mask of Anarchy*. New York: University Press, 1999.

Harper, Douglas. "American Colonization Society." In *Slavery in the North* (2003), http://www.slavenorth.com/colonize.htm.

Kuralt, Charles. *A Life on the Road*. New York: Ivy Books, 1990.

Levitt, Jeremy I. *The Evolution of Deadly Conflict in Liberia*. Durham: Carolina Academic Press, 2005.

Lithwick, Dahlia, with Madeleine Brand. "Slate's Jurisprudence: Repressed Memories and the Courts." NPR Special. 2 February 2005, http://www.npr.org/templates/story/ story.php?storyId=4490707.

McLaughlin, Abraham. "Mercy vs. justice as Liberia heals itself: Liberia's new Truth and Reconciliation Commission seeks a balance between punishment and forgiveness." *Christian Science Monitor* (26 October 2006), http://www.csmonitor.com/2006/1026/p12s01-woaf.html.

Mungeon, Donna. Interview by Noah Adams. "What Do You Take When the House Is Burning Down?" *All Things Considered.* NPR. 28 October 1993.

Nmoma, Veronica. "The Civil War and the Refugee Crisis in Liberia." *The Journal of Conflict Studies* 17/1 (Spring 1997), http://www.lib.unb.ca/Texts/JCS/bin/get.cgi?directory=SPR97/articles/&filename=nmoma.html.

Paye-Layleh, Jonathan. "Liberia President officially launches post-conflict Truth and Reconciliation Commission." AP Worldstream news release. 22 June 2006.

"Population and the Environment." Day of 6 Billion Information Kit, http://www.unfpa.org/6billion/ccmc/environment.html, September 1999.

Stone, Dan N., Ben Wier, and Stephanie M. Bryant. "Reducing Materialism Through Financial Literacy." *The CPA Journal Online* 78/2 (February 2008): http://www. nysscpa.org/cpajournal/2008/208/perspectives/p12.htm.

Tullock, John H. *The Old Testament Story.* Upper Saddle River NJ: Prentice Hall, 1999.

Warren, Rick. *The Purpose Driven Life.* Grand Rapids: Zondervan, 1995.

Wiley, Bill I. *Slaves No More—Letters from Liberia.* Lexington: University Press of Kentucky, 1980.

Williams, Gabriel. *Liberia: Heart of Darkness.* St. Victoria: Trafford Publishing, 2002.